JEET KUNE DO
THE PRINCIPLES OF A COMPLETE FIGHTER

BY: RON BALICKI
WITH DR. STEVEN GOLD

JEET KUNE DO
THE PRINCIPLES OF A COMPLETE FIGHTER

BY: RON BALICKI
WITH DR. STEVEN GOLD

FORWARD BY: DAN INOSANTO

Featuring:
P. Aslaksen, J.R. Benson, B.D. Santos, Dan Inosanto, Diana Inosanto,
M. Mukatis, M. Olsen, E. Talbot, L. Thompson and F. Valencia.

Photography by: E. Heath (Santa Monica, Los Angeles)

Editor: L. St. Clair

Publisher/Producer: FMK Rafiq

International Standard Book No: 09531766-3-0

Published/Produced by:
HNL Publishing , 5918 Fort Hamilton Parkway, Brooklyn, New York, 11219 USA

Printed by: Sanon Printing Co

Distributed by:
USA & Canada: SCB Distributors (Los Angeles)
UK & Europe: ABC (London)
Australia: Zen Imports (Sydney)

Disclaimer: Neither the author nor the publisher assumes any responsibility in any manner whatsoever for any injury which may occur by reading, following the instructions herein. Consult your physician before following any of the activities.

DEDICATION

This book is dedicated first to my Sifu, Dan Inosanto for his guidance along the martial path. Because of you I am a perpetual student. To my beautiful wife, Diana Lee Inosanto, who stands by me and inspires me to reach and surpass my goals. I am incomplete without you.

To my parents, Ron and Sylvia, thanks for having me. And of course to Sigung Bruce Lee, you have changed my life in the most positive ways; God I wish I knew you.

Thanks to Eric Paulson, for helping me get this book started. You are a great friend. Also thanks to Sue Adler-Gold for her support in the making of this book.

I want to thank everyone who helped make this book possible: Phil Aslaksen, JR Benson, Bob Delos Santos, Mike Mukatis, Mark Olsen, Ed Talbot, Lynn Thompson, Felix Valencia, Photographer - Eric Heath

And a special thanks to Larry St.Clair who dedicated so much time to designing this book.

In memory of Zoran.

Ron Balicki

— TABLE OF CONTENTS —

I am looking forward to the completion of Ron Balicki's book "JKD The Principles of a complete fighter". This book should lend more insight into the principles of Bruce Lee's Jeet Kune Do. It is essential that a student in Jeet Kune Do has a good foundation in the art of Jun Fan Gung Fu before he explores, researches and expands his own personal path of Jeet Kune Do.

A good system of martial arts encourages research, exploration and creativity among their students. Truth in the martial arts, as in life, is derived from self discovery. Each student must depart on his or her own journey to find what is workable for them in philosophy, techniques, tactics, strategies and principles and then explore other methods that interest them. Ron Balicki being a long time student understands this and this book will reflect this. Ron Balicki has been a student of mine since the early 1980's. He has instructor status under me in three separate martial arts and is one of the few people in the United States that have attained that status.

1. Jun Fan Gung Fu, Jeet Kune Do
2. The Majapaihit Martial Arts
3. The Filipino Martial Arts

In addition he has instructor rank in Shoot Wrestling under Sensei Yori Nakamura and an instructorship in Muay Thai under Ajarn (Master) Chai Sirisute. With this background he knows that there are many paths and ways in developing a fighter.

Dan Inosanto

This book is intended as a conceptual guide to Jeet Kune Do and the martial arts in general. There is only one man live certified by Sigung (founder) Bruce Lee to teach his art of The Tao of Chinese Gung Fu, Jun Fan Gung Fu and Jeet Kune Do - Sifu Dan Inosanto. Taky Kumura was certified in Jun Fan Gung Fu, not Jeet Kune Do. Simply put, this book is about the concepts Sifu Dan Inosanto taught me.

But let me back up. There are structural constraints on anything we do. Every "game" we play has its rules. For our purposes, let's distinguish between objective and subjective structural constraints.

In the martial arts, objective constraints involve the external environment. When the ground is icy or wet we have a greater chance of the fight going to the ground. It makes sense, then, that those living in icy climates need to think more about ground fighting in this regard. It is not surprising to see the forms of combat developed in the tight spaces of the Hong Kong alleyways (wing chun) differ greatly from the forms developed in the wide-open spaces of the Chinese north. The external environment will always constrain what one can do in a fight.

Subjective constraints, on this way of looking at things, involve those of the body. A person of slight build, who is tall and agile, will have an easier time with high kicks and long-range techniques. A person with a lower leg disability and great upper body strength will tend to favor more powerful close range grappling. Who we are determines what we can do.

Martial arts is a game like any other. It must be played, and played by people. Each person will play it differently. But more importantly, every game has its rules, and these rules tend to favor certain things. Basketball will favor tall people. There will be the exception, but in the main, the way the game is played will tend to favor people who can jump, block and score over another.

Sifu Inosanto always said that martial arts was a bit like a menu. You and your friends may order from the same menu, and look at the same set of choices, but it should not be a surprise when each person orders something to his or her own taste. These same kinds of rules will apply in the martial arts. Hence the purpose of this book. It is our intent to lay out these rules, to expose the underlying concepts that structure our experience as martial artists, and the concepts taught to me by Sifu Inosanto.

To my mind, JKD is the art of researching and developing these attributes. JKD is not a system; it is not a style. Bruce Lee rejected the notion of "style" as it necessarily brought on ossification. When martial artists pledge allegiance to a style they tend to see it as complete and in need of little or no modification. They tend to defend the style dogmatically. Then, when they find another fighter that they cannot deal with, they panic. How can their "complete" "perfect" "best in the world" style be beaten? What do we do now?

JKD seeks the opposite. This may seem like an odd thing to say, but a true JKD player seeks out failure. A true JKD player looks for the situation that s/he does not know how to deal with. Then, when the situation is met, s/he looks for a solution. By repeatedly finding internal weaknesses, and then finding solutions, the JKD player improves as a fighter and becomes a better person. This constant need to grow by testing limits takes a very secure person. Anyone feels better clinging to the illusion that he or she has all the answers. It is not easy to let go and realize that you can be beaten. But, in this humility the only path to self-perfection lies.

If JKD is clearly the "way of no way", the "style of no style" then why do so many JKD players insist that they have the "true" art of JKD, that they are preserving the "authentic" art developed by Bruce Lee? It would seem, if you really read Bruce right, that there is no such thing as "authentic" JKD - there is no "style" to preserve. JKD, Bruce Lee said, must be a creation of the individual.

Each of us seeks our own way. So why the regression to the calcified codified "art" the founder so vehemently detested? In our view, it has nothing to do with Bruce Lee and everything to do with power.

The modern French postructuralist philosopher Michel Foucault said that "knowledge is power". He did not mean, as is so often said in popular culture, that if you have knowledge you will get power. Quite the opposite is the case. For Foucault this statement is an identity statement - knowledge equals power. Foucault tells us that knowledge is developed as a means of control. Nowhere is there a better example of this than in contemporary JKD debates. Think of it this way, if you have the "true" knowledge, if you know what Bruce Lee "really" meant, then you are the one people will come to for lessons. No one sells magazines like Bruce Lee. No one in the martial arts world has a more magnetic draw. If a martial artist can play off of that, by claiming to have the only true knowledge, then people will come to him to learn. Underneath this wholesale abandonment of the master's philosophy is the desire for power. Those who claim to know the "true JKD art" are really about money. There is no such thing as the "true JKD art". That is why we are not telling you that this book is the "how to" book of JKD. We are not saying that we have the correct techniques. However, there are certain principles and there are certain concepts Bruce Lee developed. Each person will fill in the blanks differently. Each person will take the concepts and create an art that works for them. We can only help to expose just what those concepts are.

BIOS

Ron Balicki grew up in the windy city of Chicago. Awe struck with Bruce Lee, Ron was inspired to study the martial arts. After indepth study of the martial arts, Ron sought out the one man who truly understood Bruce Lee's teachings, Sifu Dan Inosanto. After many years of study, Ron earned his instructorship in Jun Fan Gung fu (Jeet Kune Do Concepts) and Filipino Kali from Sifu Inosanto. In 1987 Ron became a Cook County Deputy Sheriff stationed in Chicago, IL. Ron helped form the Cook County Sheriffs Special Operations Resistance Team (S.O.R.T.) - a team of officers trained to do riot control. At this time Ron also began work as a body-

Ron bodyguarding action movie star Steven Seagal.

guard for various Hollywood movie and music stars. Ron went on to obtain an instructorship in Maphilindo Silat from Sifu Inosanto. He also has earned instructorships in Shoot Wrestling, under the undefeated middleweight Shoot Wrestling Champion Yorinaga Nakamura, Thai Boxing under Ajarn (Master) Surchai Sirisute, Wing Chun Gung Fu under Sifu Randy Williams, Bullwhip (Latigo Y' Daga) instructor under Tom Meadows and Anthony DeLongis. Ron also received the rank of Senior Assistant Instructor under the late Punong Guro (Head Instructor) Edgar G. Sulite in the art of Lameco Escrima. Ron is a third degree black belt under Fred Degerberg, owner of the world famous Degerberg Academy in Chicago, IL.

In 1993 Ron moved to Los Angeles to take on the job of instructor and manager of the Inosanto Academy of Martial Arts. Ron fought full contact stick fighting competitions and fought professionally in Shoot Wrestling competitions in Japan and America. Ron continues to learn from many instructors in many styles of the martial arts, traveling to Indonesia and beyond. Military, Law Enforcement, Anti-Terrorist groups and the French President's Secret Service all have sought Ron out for experience and teaching skills. Ron is the author of numerous articles for magazines worldwide, and has produced a widely respected series of training videos.

Dr. Steven Gold has been a private "garage" student of Ron Balicki's for the past five years. Studying Jun Fan Gungfu, Kali, and whatever else Ron throws at him, he particularly enjoys, trapping, chi sao, and the wooden dummy. Dr. Gold also writes free lance for different martial arts magazines.

At his day job, Dr. Gold is an Associate Professor of Business Administration and Health Sciences at Touro University International where he teaches management theory, Information technology, and liberal arts. Dr. Gold received his Bachelor's degree in Political Science and History from the University of California at Los Angeles, and his Master's and Ph.D. degrees in Philosophy from the University of California at Santa Barbara. He taught philosophy, politics, ethics, classics, and law at Carleton College in Minnesota, Iowa State University, and Southern Connecticut State University.

Dr. Gold is the author of three books on ethics and public policy, and political/legal theory, as well as dozens of articles in philosophy, information technology, ethics, politics, business, and law.

1 —————————— INTRODUCTION

In some sense, writing a book on Jeet Kune Do is a presumptuous thing to do. Entering into a discussion about the work of the master may seem absurd when the master himself clearly said:

> *If people say Jeet Kune Do is different from "this" or from "that,"*
> *then let the name of Jeet Kune Do be wiped out, for that is what it is,*
> *just a name. Please don't fuss over it.* (208)

Of course, this may just be the greatest expression of modesty in the 20th century. It is more than worth fussing over Jeet Kune Do. But I don't think that this statement should be taken as an injunction against writing a book like this. First, and foremost, this passage is really more about politics than about philosophy. Bruce Lee warns against setting up camps, creating competing schools, and fighting over who has the "true" JKD lineage. This is wise. But just as important, Bruce Lee provokes a sense of modesty in anyone who wishes to do philosophy and discuss the nature of JKD. Sure we should fuss over what we mean when we say that we are JKD players. However, we simply need to be very careful about what we are doing.

The objectives for writing a book like this are best set out by Linda Lee in the introduction to the Tao of Jeet Kune Do:

> *He did not intend it to be a "how-to" book...*
> *He intended it as a record of one man's way of thinking and as a*
> *guide, not a set of instructions.*

In that spirit I present this book. I do not presume to create the definitive interpretation of Bruce Lee's thought. Nor do I pretend to create a "how-to" book that will show the true JKD way of fighting. This book simply represents an honest attempt at presenting some of the results of my many years of martial arts exploration in the JKD tradition. I've walked the JKD path for a long time and this is what I have found. If you find it helpful, if you can absorb something that is useful, then the time taken out to write this book will have been time well spent.

THE METAPHYSICS OF JEET KUNE DO

The best way to begin thinking about Jeet Kune Do lies on the level of metaphysics. There seems to be a sense among many practitioners that JKD is a thing that exists somewhere - being as a thing in a state of perfection to be preserved. On this view, we must take care of the "original" and "true" JKD as the prophet revealed it. In my view, nothing could be further from the truth.

When I first came to the Inosanto Academy, Sifu Dan had this 'inexpensive' little wood frame that hung on the wall. It had curtains covering the front of it with a sign that said, "the truth of JKD lies behind this curtain". When you would pull the curtain back, it would reveal a mirror - a mirror that obviously reflected the face of the one who pulled the chord. This frame is long gone. But the message remains. JKD lives in its practitioners. There is no such thing as JKD independent of the people who practice the art. For Bruce Lee, and for those who follow his lead, martial arts is an intensely individual experience. Each of us creates JKD in his or her own way.

This radical subjectivism is not as unusual as it might seem. Think for a moment about physical conditioning; something closely related to martial arts training. Each of us approaches conditioning differently. Each of us conditions given the advantages and limitations of our body and our life. Some of us are better set up for swimming and running. Others find weights, sparring, and bicycling as the path to physical health. But no matter how one approaches the matter, the results are inherently subjective. We build our own bodies. There is no such thing as "fitness" out there as a pure phenomenon to strive for. "Fitness" is then supervenient in that the concept will instantiate itself diff-erently in each person. To see "fitness" as a singular external phenomenon, with a singular path to achieve that state, is to miss the nature of the animal. And yet, this is the approach of the traditional martial artist - and the folly of many modern JKD players.

This subjectivist phenomenology stands in stark contrast to the traditional approach where the style is more important than the practitioner. In the Tao of Jeet Kune Do, Bruce Lee says that,

...in classical styles, system becomes more important than the man!
The classical man functions with the pattern of a style! (18)

For the classical man, style determines the person. Modern JKD players should not make the same mistake. To assume that the style exists beyond the individual, to assume that the style manifests itself in a manner more important than the practitioner, is to forget the existential nature of the JKD phenomenon.

In some sense, then, there is no such thing, or better, no such style, as Jeet Kune Do. Bruce Lee says,

Jeet Kune Do favors formlessness so that it can assume all forms and
since Jeet Kune Do has no style, it can fit in with all styles. As a result,
Jeet Kune Do utilizes all ways and is bound by none and, likewise,
uses any techniques or means which serve its end. (12)

JKD has no form and has no content. It is a way. Fundamentally this comes from the dynamic metaphysics embraced by Bruce Lee. He categorically rejects the static notion of form. In order to make sense of reality and respond to the physical challenges it brings, we must be dynamic.

Having totality means being capable of following "what is," because
"what is" is constantly moving and constantly changing. If one is
anchored to a particular view, one will not be able to follow the swift
movement of "what is." (18)

Let's be clear however, that this emphasis on a dynamic metaphysic comes about for very practical reasons. This is not simply abstract ontological speculation.
When, in a split second, your life is threatened, do you say, "Let me

make sure my hand is on my hip, and my style is "the style"? When
your life is in danger, do you argue about the method you will adhere
to while saving yourself? Why the duality? (22)

Bruce Lee rejected the duality of method versus reaction. Rather, he suggests

STYLE

that a completely dynamic flow brings style and action together and makes for
the complete fighter. JKD is experience; JKD is activity. As such, JKD is not a
style to be preserved; it is a way of becoming.

Bruce Lee clearly rejected the basic notion of a singular correct all-encompass-
ing "style". He based his eclecticism on the rejection of duality mentioned
above, but a functional rejection of duality specifically. He says,

Please do not be concerned with soft versus firm, kicking versus
striking, grappling versus hitting and kicking, long-range fighting
versus in-fighting. There is no such thing as "this" is better than
"that". Should there be one thing we must guard against, let it be
partiality that robs us of our pristine wholeness and makes us lose
unity in the midst of duality. (23)

The rejection is functional in that he defines the art in terms of success. "In this
art, efficiency is anything that scores". (24) There is no singular style that leads
to winning. Style is whatever wins. For example, few things could be more eso-
teric and less directly practical than the game of chi sao. And yet, Bruce Lee
continued to practice the game he learned from his Wing Chun roots. When one
gets to the higher levels of chi sao, it can develop tremendous sensitivity. The
tactile response chi sao develops can directly help a fighter "score". As such,
though it is the most arcane of games, it is "efficient" and can be well worth the
time.

Let me further emphasize this point - JKD does not reject forms. It does not
reject classical training. If forms training will help you "score" then it can be a
good sort of thing. However, the true expression of art, the emoting of martial
truth, comes from a development beyond form. Bruce Lee said that:

Expression is not developed through the practice of form, yet form is a part of expression. There greater (expression) is found in the lesser (expression) but the lesser is found within the greater. Having "no form" then, does not mean having no "form". Having "no form" evolves from having form. "No form" is the higher individual expression. (25)

JKD reflects the individual. The individual is a product of action. So JKD is a product of action. The individual is alive, so JKD is alive.

Saying that JKD rejects static classical notions, given that they do not reflect the natural active reality of fighting, is, in some sense, not that controversial. But Bruce Lee was careful to warn against those who get carried away with this perspective.

Do not deny the classical approach simply as a reaction, for you will have created another pattern and trapped yourself there. (25)

A simple rejection of forms and classical training is no better than the trap of classical training itself. Whatever is useful must be absorbed. And this includes classical forms, to the extent that they give the fighter an edge. I will have more to say on this in the sections on training and trapping.

Bruce Lee very clearly rejected static, academic, notions. However, one must TEACH. Teaching, as an activity, is an odd sort of thing. The LIVE activity of

JKD PEDAGOGY

fighting must be reduced to static textbook, read academic, material. What is a live flow must now have definable points, for pedagogical purposes. There might be seven points in a knife flow drill. You can hear the instructor shouting out 1, 2, 3....as you cleanly and sharply hit each point. But this is an illusion. In fact, the flow moves without stopping; there is no "point" to define it.

Look at it another way: as the hand covers the line from the face to the shoulder, Biu Jee blends into Jong Sao, which in turn slides into Tan Sao (see photos A,B,C in Chapter 6). Yes, Biu, Jong, and Tan are definably different hand motions, each with a proper structure. These different motions must be

learned and the structure developed properly. We separate Biu, from Jong, from Tan in order to isolate the moves and make sure they are learned properly, that is effectively. But in reality, when the movement comes alive, there is no distinction.

The opponent throws a left hook. Your right hand comes up to block. The point at which your hand meets the incoming strike determines which defending movement comes out. If you catch it quickly, in deep, a Biu Sao comes out. If the attacking hand is caught later, a Tan Sao happens. Caught mid way, and a Jong occurs. In reality, when the punch is thrown, the defender must cover the line. Which block is used to cover the line is determined, not by choice, not by rational decision-making, but by reaction. One does not think "this is coming in a little too close to my face for a Jong Sao. I think I will use a Tan". No, with proper training, the Tan simply happens. More importantly, at what point in the defensive arc from Biu to Tan does the Jong cease to be a Jong and become a Tan? It doesn't. In reality, in activity - where JKD can be found - there is no difference.

With this said, we can see the duality between teaching and fighting. Teaching is an academic exercise. It is often, by necessity, a dead sort of thing. In order to teach tan Sao properly one must break the activity of covering the line into three static parts. One can diagram it, put numbers on it, and generally give the movement a static fixed expression. However, when the real fight happens, one must let go of the static. When the art comes alive, these distinctions become artificial. Probably the single greatest challenge then, when teaching from a JKD perspective, is to bear in mind that teaching forces us to take the live art and make it non-living - take the active and make it static. This is fine for the purposes of learning correct theory and structure. But it must be taken for what it is worth, a learning experience.

ECLECTICISM AND SIMPLICITY

What we are seeing with JKD, then, is a commitment to everything and nothing. Much has been made of Bruce Lee's rejection of connections to a singular style. JKD is all styles and none. JKD players are eclectic. But the "jack of all trades, master of none" criticism really does not obtain. Speaking for myself, I reached fairly sophisticated levels in a number of traditional arts. This is a good sort of thing. Many in the JKD way overstate the imperative to "strip away" tradition. In order to chip away at the stone, the sculptor must have some stone to

work with. The potter throws more clay as he or she shapes the pot. A JKD player explores and tests every promising martial art, exploring in depth.

As one explores other arts, the litmus test for deciding what to keep and what to throw away is simplicity. Bruce Lee says that,

> *Jeet Kune Do does not beat around the bush. It does not take winding detours. It follows a straight line to the objective. Simplicity is the shortest distance between two points.* (12)

The decision procedure for absorbing what is useful lies in notion of simplicity. What scores will inevitably be the simplest means to an end. We are reminded of the ancient imperative known as Ockham's razor. Simply put, when two or more explanations serve to adequately describe the phenomenon, always choose the simplest. It is this kind of commitment to finding the most direct explanation, the shortest distance between two points, that directs us towards the techniques that produce success.

I have always felt that, to really do JKD, one must be a very secure person.

THE SECURE FIGHTER

The path of JKD is the path of rooting out ignorance, meeting the task, and overcoming the challenge. This may seem like an odd thing to say, but the real JKD player looks for failure. If a person only seeks out success, only looks for things that s/he can win at, he or she will never improve. The essence of improvement lies in facing our shortcomings straight on and finding solutions.

This takes a very secure person. No one wants to look foolish. No one wants to lose. This is particularly acute for the marital arts instructor. Much of the instructor's credibility is based on reputation and appearance.

Ron during a Pro Shooto Fight in Tokyo - 1997

Students come to the master who seems undefeatable, who has all the answers. If a martial arts instructor fails in front of students, they may take their business elsewhere. But nothing could be more dangerous. The instructor, who always sets it up so s/he will always win, who never faces failure, will never grow as an artist. Bruce Lee says that,

> *Learning Jeet Kune Do is not a matter of seeking knowledge or accumulating stylized pattern, but is discovering the cause of ignorance.* (208)

But there is more to it than merely appearances, and even attitude. The willingness to throw off the comforting so-called "truths" of traditional styles takes the kind of person who is willing to boldly face the void of uncertainty. Bruce Lee says,

> *To express yourself in freedom, you must die to everything of yesterday. From the "old", you derive security; form the "new", you gain the flow.* (16)

Dying to everything you know, freeing yourself from the "old", is an intimidating process. The old comfortable routines of tradition give a sense of security - a false sense of security. Though we may be told that "this has always worked in the past", if you don't test it yourself you don't know if it is a myth perpetuated by mistake, or truly effective. The JKD player must be secure in the knowledge of his or her abilities in order to be willing to test everything and take nothing for granted.

Bruce Lee took this even further. To really 'gain the flow' one must even free oneself from a notion that the real "truth" comes from JKD itself:

> *For security, the unlimited living is turned into something dead, a chosen pattern that limits. To understand Jeet Kune Do, one ought to throw away all ideals, patterns, styles; in fact, we should throw away even the concepts of what is or isn't ideal in Jeet Kune Do.* (11)

If we create JKD as a new "style", with all the same types of set patterns and ideals, we have done nothing more than create a new cage.

THE BUSINESS OF MARTIAL ARTS

Personally, I would like to take this even one step further, and relate it to the business of martial arts in the modern world of competitive capitalism. Having "The Truth" sells. Knowledge is power. And by this I don't mean the simplistic ideal that, if you have knowledge you will get power. I am aiming at something deeper. If I "know" the only way to win a fight, if I have the exclusive "recipe" for success, then you have to pay ME to learn it. The martial artist who says, "I have the one and only, best, complete, martial style that is guaranteed to win" aims for power over the marketplace. In truth, the whole mystique built around many martial arts 'masters' today lays in a grand marketing scheme. But this is an illusion. Bruce Lee says,

> *Just as yellow leaves may be gold coins to stop the crying children,*
> *thus, the so-called secret moves and contorted postures appease the*
> *unknowledgeable marital artists.* (19)

Pick up any martial arts magazine and you will see long advertisements, presented like real articles, which claim to have an unstoppable secret. "Punch so fast it is invisible!". "Learn the secrets even Navy Seals don't know!" Absurd, I know. But this is only the extreme of the phenomenon. The same mentality can be seen in serious reputable martial artists.

In the 1990's, a wave of grappling enthusiasm swept the United States and beyond. Some of the finest grapplers came to the US to sell their wares. I studied with a number of them and have the deepest respect for their talents and styles. However, some of the most pernicious myths have been perpetuated for just this sort of financial reason. How often have we heard the claim that "all fights will of necessity go the ground"? Since all fights immediately go to the ground, one must learn from the best ground fighters in the world, and not bother with other arts that emphasize stand up fighting and weapons. The first part of this claim is only a partial truth.

Most streetfights will go to the ground at some point. But not all do, and this is not always the preferred method of fighting. Those who restrict themselves solely to unarmed ground fighting neglect other extremely important areas needed for self-defense.

Worse yet, the myth that all fights immediately go to the ground leads to the outright untruth that one cannot face multiple attackers. Later on in this book I will show a number of techniques for facing multiple attackers. The claim that multiple attackers are unbeatable represents a myth put forward to deal with the obvious inadequacy of a system based solely on ground fighting. If these ground systems cannot account for multiple attackers - and it is hard to take three people to the ground at once - then they are not complete systems and one must look elsewhere to learn. However, as a means of keeping the corner on martial arts knowledge, (done often honestly and with the best of intentions) the popular ground fighting schools perpetuate this myth. This is a dangerous way to do mass marketing.

The honest martial artist must admit that the security of the complete, undefeatable, martial arts system is a pernicious and simplistic illusion that is hard to let go. Bruce Lee says,

Fear comes from uncertainty. When we are absolutely certain, whether of our worth or our worthlessness, we are almost impervious to fear. Thus a feeling of utter unworthiness can be a source of courage. Everything seems possible when we are absolutely helpless or absolutely powerful - and both states stimulate our gullibility. (205)

The truly secure person who can embrace Jeet Kune Do knows that there is no secret style, no one true way to do everything. The path of JKD is a path of uncovering personal ignorance, of meeting failure head on and overcoming the fear that this uncertainty creates. Doing this takes an exceptionally secure sort of person.

JKD AND ETHICS

To conclude this introductory section on JKD theory we must bring it home to the personal. Jeet Kune Do is more than just a way of looking at the fight. It is an ethic. To really become a JKD player one must...

...destroy anything bothering your mind. Not to hurt anyone, but to overcome your own greed, anger and folly. Jeet Kune Do is directed toward oneself. (13)

JKD is as much about personal moral improvement as it is about fighting. Only in the western world do we distinguish moral character from self-defense. Bruce Lee's mission lay in bringing the Chinese way of thinking to Western audiences, be it through movies, television or print. Of course he told us much about conditioning the body. But, like the Taoism so prevalent in his work, Bruce Lee rejected the Cartesian dualism inherent in the Western zeitgeist.

Ethics, martial arts and family all come together. Ron and Diana Lee Inosanto on their wedding day. From left: Sue Inosanto, Dan Inosanto, Diana Lee Inosanto and their son Sebatian, Ron Balicki Jr., Ron Balicki, Sr., Sylvia Balicki.

You cannot, on Bruce Lee's way of seeing things, be a good fighter, be a well-conditioned athlete, without developing your personal character at the same time. He says that,

Self-knowledge is the basis of Jeet Kune Do because it is effective, not only for the individual's marital art, but also for his life as a human being. (208)

Facing uncertainty, learning to be secure, seeking out and overcoming failure, being honest in the challenges you face are virtues as much concerned with the human condition as with the way of fighting. Integrating the person into the fight, locating the art in the individual, not the abstract style, makes Jeet Kune Do a way of life as well as a way of martial training. And it is precisely this element of character that brought me to JKD in the first place.

Note: all passages are quoted from Bruce Lee's The Tao of Jeet Kune Do.

By far, the greatest challenge to a teacher lies in making it real. How do we make training replicate actual combat such that, when the real thing happens, the right response comes out? To be sure, this does not mean that we always need to rely on realistic actual fighting. While sparring has a crucial role to play in realistic training, the right kinds of training equipment can allow the instructor to isolate particular elements of the fight and train them directly, practically, and realistically.

Dan Inosanto introduced focus mitts to Bruce Lee in the early '60's, and the gloves quickly found a signature niche in the JKD repertoire. A focus mitt looks like a large open padded glove with a white dot in the open palm for a target. The focus mitts allow the instructor to simulate real fight scenarios in at least two ways. First, the mitt, given the thickness, allows the practitioner to "unload" on

his opponent. The student can hit a focus mitt much harder than he or she will likely do in sparring or competition, and certainly much harder than he or she would in any other classroom activity. This allows the student to hit realistically, as hard as he or she likes, without fear of hurting the other person or even hurting him or herself, and with a great degree of accuracy. Second, focus mitts allow the instructor to really put pressure on the student. The speed at which the instructor moves the workout, and the pressure he or she can put on the student, is quite dramatic. Going "all out", with focus mitt drills, trains pragmatically and helps keep the student healthy and prepared in those crucial days before a fight.

Most martial artists use the focus mitts at one range, two at most. Bruce Lee created a system where focus mitts are used at all ranges (long, medium, close (i.e., trapping) and ground fighting). During training, while holding the mitts, Bruce Lee broke away from the static posture typical of the trainer, instead preferring to employ focus mitts in a dynamic way. Lee would attack the student and force him or her to work the different ranges. The solid focus mitt, then, makes for realistic training at all ranges.

Much like the focus mitts, I have found Thai Pads to exhibit the same pedagogical virtues. Though Bruce Lee himself did not use them, they can be used for the same desiderata exhibited by focus mitts. Thai pads build power. Thai pads deliver an excellent anaerobic workout. I use them to condition fighters, teach them to deal with speed and power, and to help them simulate elements of real combat by "unloading" with all they have.

The Wooden Dummy, or Mook Jong, certainly has a special place in my heart and in the training of many of my students. Bruce Lee brought the dummy along from his early training in Wing Chun Gung Fu. The dummy, a telephone pole like body with three arms facing out, and a crooked leg at the bottom, is used to build sensitivity, technique, and to condition.

The wood obviously conditions the arms. Hitting a solid piece of wood, even pine (though most use hardwoods), develops strength and durability in the fighter. But even more importantly, the dummy emphasizes good form. The dummy acts something like a protractor. It forces the practitioner to pay attention to proper angles. If you strike the dummy at the wrong angle, you will feel it. The bruises and goose eggs new students see on their arms derive as much from hitting the dummy wrong, and being forced into the correct angles, as they come from an unconditioned arm hitting the wood. Furthermore, the wooden dummy teaches excellent forward pressure. Proper form dictates that techniques be pressed into the opponent. And the dummy is a great way to learn.

Bruce Lee was a strong believer in striking targets. He would use pads, paper, and even other people for target practice. Paper was always one of his favorites. There will be no hesitation when hitting a hanging piece of paper. And yet, paper lets you visualize in an explosive manner. You can explode out at a piece of paper without any concern. When striking a pad the practitioner will typically hold back and not release his or her full power. Some worry about injuring their hands, others have trouble visualizing. Paper allows the practitioner to get the full value of target practice while applying full throttle.

Of course, as someone who has done quite a bit of boxing, I also advocate the use of the bag. It is no secret that Bruce Lee admired and emulated boxers like Muhammad Ali. Punching bags offer a vehicle to develop timing. Speed bags, in particular, develop coordination and rhythm. Heavier bags allow the practitioner to develop power. Heavier bags are ideal to develop conditioning and stamina. And finally, using a bag allows for the development of a flowing motion. Working techniques on a bag will get the practitioner to move and flow while really pushing hard.

Equipment training was one of Bruce Lee's fortes. He was amazingly creative. Dan Inosanto was responsible for brining many of the different pieces of equipment to Bruce Lee's attention. He introduced Bruce to football shields, focus mitts, and even convinced him to give up running in combat boots in favor of track shoes. But it was Bruce Lee who took that equipment and found creative ways to use it to sharpen JKD attributes. This open minded approach to equipment training should inspire us to experiment and test out every kind of training devices that seems promising.

Ron and Mike face off

Mike jabs and Ron parries

1 - Mike crosses; Ron parries the cross and inside Eye jabs (Loy Biu Gee) Mike

2 - Ron crosses

Inside Entry Against The Cross

3 - Hooks

4 - Crosses and...

5 - Round kicks

JUN FAN GUNG FU
FOCUS MITT DRILLS

Outside Entry Against The Cross

4 - Hooks and...

3 - Crosses

5 - Round kicks

Ron and Mike face off

Mike jabs and Ron parries

2 - Ron hooks

1 - Mike crosses; Ron parries the cross and
outside Eye jabs (Noy Biu Gee) Mike

Jun Fan Gung Fu Focus Mitt Drills

Split Entry With Jow Sao Against The Jab

5 - Ron Knees and...

4 - Ron pulls Mike's arms down
(Seung Jut Sao)

6 - Elbows

Ron and Mike face off

1 - Mike jabs and Ron parries and
punches between Mike's arms

3 - Ron hooks Mike; Mike uses his arm
to cover

2 - Ron swings his left arm to the outside
(Jow Sao)

Jun Fan Gung Fu
Focus Mitt Drills

Split Entry With Jow Sao To Takedown Finish

4 - Ron pulls Mike's arms down (Seung Jut Sao)

Ron and Mike face off

1 - Mike jabs and Ron parries and punches between Mike's arms

2 - Ron swings his left arm to the outside (Jow Sao)

3 - Ron hooks Mike; Mike uses his arm to cover

5a - Ron goes in for a hip throw and...

5b - Ron takes Mike to the ground

6 - Ron puts his knee on Mike's stomach...

7 - Puts his leg over Mike's head and...

8 - Lays back into a straight arm bar

JUN FAN GUNG FU FOCUS MITT DRILLS

Jun Fan Gung Fu Empty Hand And Focus Mitt Comparisons

A1

Ron and Mike face off

B1

A2

Ron jabs, Mike parries

B2

A3

Ron crosses;

B3

A4

Mike parries the cross

B4

A5

Ron grabs and pulls (Lap Sao) Mike's arm and...

B5

A6

B6

Backhand strikes Mike

A7

B7

Ron hooks

A8

B8

Crosses

A9   Ron hooks   B9

A10   Round kicks   B1

FOCUS MITT DRILLS

Hip Check - Empty Hand And Focus Mitt Comparisons

A1

Ron jabs at Marc

B1

A2

Marc double leg tackles Ron, but Ron thrusts his hip
forward stalling Marc's forward momentum

B2

A3

Ron crosses

B3

A4

Hooks

B4

A5

And left kicks.

B5

FOCUS MITT DRILLS

Stiff Arm - Empty Hand And Focus Mitt Comparisons

A1

Ron kicks Marc; Marc covers and...

B1

A2

Marc tries to double leg tackle Ron; Ron stiff-arms
Marc stopping his forward momentum

B2

A3

Ron crosses

B3

A4

Hooks and...

B4

A5

Left round kicks Marc.

B5

. . .

Weapons are the great equalizer. One person with a weapon, who knows how to use it, is as good as two. A smaller person with a weapon stands a much greater chance against a larger opponent when he or she is armed. As such, JKD players tend to be open to experimentation with different weapons. Anything that can give you an edge is a good sort of thing. Learning to use as a weapon whatever you can find lying about is really a standard principle in martial arts training. To my mind, the most common things you will find are sticks and blades. Sharp edged materials and stick like objects are everywhere. So learning to use the stick and the knife are among the most practical things you can do. And yet, there is more to weapons training than this direct pragmatic imperative. The stick itself is used mostly for training. But it can be lethal. One of the inter-

THE STICK

esting aspects of the stick is that it allows you to hurt to a degree. You can control the amount of damage you do in a way that you cannot with a blade weapon. The right kind of stick can shatter bone. A blade cuts; and that is a good thing mind you. But a stick can destroy - to a greater or lesser degree.

I first learned Filipino martial arts with the stick. The Filipinos believe that, if you can build a fast confident reaction to the stick, if you can go 100+mph, then the empty hand will follow. In some martial systems, weapons represent extremely advanced applications of empty hand techniques. But, in the Filipino system, the weapon logically comes first. Stick drills create speed and sharpen timing. You learn how to use your whole body for not only striking with the stick itself, but punching as well. The application to empty hands then is direct and practical.

Ron (left) with Grand Master Leo Giron (center) Joel Clark (right), 1994

The double stick drill is called sinawali (weaving). It teaches the student to be ambidextrous. With sinawali, in a short time you will accumulate so many repetitions that you will be flowing quickly. The amount of repetitions, and the speed, allows you to flow without thinking about what you are doing. The Filipino's say that the hands have minds of their own. This kind of repetition, then, allows you to act with "no mind". Like tying your shoe, the sinawali drill lets you simply react.

Training with the stick, as was said, is also quite practical. Training the stick allows you to train anything you might put in your hand, e.g., a sword, knife, umbrella, cane, book, etc.,). Furthermore, knowing how to use the stick allows you to know how to defend against it. An assailant may also pick up a stick, a cane, an umbrella, and use it as a weapon. In fact, this is the most likely scenario where an unarmed assailant spontaneously uses whatever is available to arm him or herself. It is worth, then, knowing how to respond.

The stick builds speed, coordination and timing. As a training tool, as a method for building the true attributes of a complete fighter, few, if any, things come close to the stick. The stick is directly practical. There is almost always a stick like object lying around. Knowing how to use them, and how to defend against them, is among the most practical things you can train. Knife self-defense is the hardest area for the martial arts instructor to look at honestly. In knife fighting the odds can be at their worst, and the margin for error essentially non-existent. However, I have found that compositions of the right techniques from the Filipino martial arts can substantially push things towards your favor. If you are honest and diligent in your art, work different ranges, test different arts, and train for every situation, you can significantly increase your chance of surviving a knife confrontation.

THE KNIFE

Have your ever honestly asked yourself what you would do if confronted by a knife-wielding attacker? Should you grab something and defend yourself, run, or start begging and pleading for your life? To be brutally honest, my first inclination is to run. In a knife fight there is near absolute certainty that your will be cut, and likely cut fatally. Why take the risk? Instructors, especially those who teach a wide variety of disarm techniques need to be honest with their students. Nothing could be worse than giving your student an inflated sense of self-confidence. There is no shame in running from a fight that you will almost certainly be seriously injured in. Being a former law enforcement officer I have seen the bad side of knife altercations more than I would like to remember. Defending yourself in a knife confrontation should be your course of action only after escape is impossible and you can't seem to talk your way out of it. Given the danger, your students deserve at least this much honesty right from the start. As Fred Degerberg has said:

Winners drip, losers gush.

Many martial systems offer a small section on knife self-defense, or none at all. Many instructors avoid the subject altogether. Worse yet, I have been is some classes where it is clear that the instructor is making up the defensive tactics as he goes along. This is a disaster waiting to happen! Never equip your student with untested opinions about the knife. Show what you know and end it there. Your unwillingness to show that there is something you don't know may lead to a situation where your student, brimming with unwarranted confidence, loses his or her life. This is too serious a matter for ego and posturing. Your students deserve an honest assessment of your knowledge your and limitations.

If you don't accept my premise about the dangers of knife fighting I suggest a simple exercise to prove the point. Put on a fencing mask, a white T-shirt and hand your training partner a marker. See if you can disarm the marker without getting inked up. Once you are covered with stab and slash ink marks all over you, my position will seem much more realistic.

With all this said, it may seem like there is little point in training at knife fighting. After all, if your chances of succeeding are slim, why bother? Being realistic and impressing on your students the serious danger of a knife does not mean that proper training cannot significantly increase your odds. I have found, through years of focus as a martial artist and Deputy Sheriff, that it is possible to come out on top. If you have no choice, if your tennis shoes and rhetoric fails you, then you must fight. Training for knife fighting is among the most demanding and complicated areas for a martial artist to succeed at. But it can be done.

Dexter Labonog, Ron, Sifu Inosanto, Grandmaster Leo Giron, Punong Guro Edgar Sulite, Grandmaster Tony Somera - 1994

In my experience, the best place to find practical knife techniques is in the Filipino martial arts. That is not to say that other arts don't have much to offer. Rather, my 14 years of experience under Guro Dan Inosanto in Kali, combined with 8 years of work with the late Punong Guro Edgar G. Sulite in the art of Lameco Escrima, has led me to believe that some of the most realistic and useful techniques come from the Philippines.

Filipino systems developed detailed knife methods largely because that weapon in particular is prevalent in their society. Unlike many other systems, Philippine styles kept their competitiveness due to years of colonialism. During peacetime, knife-fighting techniques have a tendency to become stylized. Unfortunately, 200 years of Spanish, and later, American rule often did not allow for a peaceful environment. In fact, the Spanish had a tendency to imprison together members of rival tribes. This inter-tribal conflict, in close quarters, led to a keen development of knife tactics and awareness.

When I teach Filipino knife fighting I weave together drills and techniques from
both Kali and Lameco
Escrima, creating not a
new system, but a new
way of looking at these
systems. Principally, I
teach what I have been
taught. However, mix-
ing drills from the
Inosanto system with
the Lameco Escrima
exercises, or 'Laban
Laro" (literally, "play
fighting"), allows me

to turn drills into play. The more game-like the drill is the easier it is to motivate
students to work. Knife fighting, in particular, demands a tremendous amount of
repetition in order to ingrain or "hard-wire" the correct movements. In knife
fighting, where there is no room for error, heightened awareness and instanta-
neous reactions are essential. Proper body placement, increased tactile awareness, training each hand equally, and the like, come quickly when the drill is
turned into a game.

One of the other major advantages for both Kali and Lameco Escrima is the
emphasis on knife fighting at all ranges. In my experience I have seen many who
refuse to work certain ranges with the knife because they feel that they can avoid
a range where they are at a disadvantage. This common mentality is patently
unrealistic. Anyone can be caught at any range at any time. Those who feel that
they will never be forced to work close range with the knife are simply deceiv-
ing themselves. One may, for example, be falsely arrested and temporarily find
oneself behind bars facing a "shank" (homemade knife) at close quarters. Similarly, a slippery or icy surface may force anyone to the ground in a knife confrontation. Any range is possible at any time. That is why I prefer to work in the
Filipino systems, where all ranges are examined.

My intention is to approach knife fighting with the honesty it deserves. Simply put, knife fighting is dangerous. However, your chances can increase if you train hard, in a realistic fashion, and in a system that allows you to create an art that is effective rather than simply aesthetic. No one art has all the answers on how to increase your odds in a knife fight. For this reason I continue to investigate more efficient ways to protect myself as well as my loved ones.

Mike and Mark square off

1 - Mark chambers his weapon hand, ready to deliver a backhand strike

2 - Mark swings a backhand strike; Mike hits Mark's hand with backhand strike

3 - Mark swings a backhand strike; Mike hits Mark's hand with backhand strike

4 - Mike follows up with a forehand strike to Mark's head.

Mike and Mark square off

1 - Mark throws a forehand strike at Mike.
Mike defends with a roof block

2 - Mike scoops Mark's weapon hand
counter clockwise grabbing firmly onto
Mark's hand at the pad of the thumb

3 - Mike places Mark's stick on his forearm
(you can also place the stick on your
biceps or waist)

KALI STICK VS. STICK DRILL
Stick Vs. Stick Technique #2

4 - Mike swings his stick at Marc disarming Mark's stick in the process

5 - Following through hitting Marc in the head.

Mike and Mark square off

1 - Mark swings a forehand strike at Mike
Mike defends by meeting Mark's strike
with a forehand hit

2 - Mike switches the stick to his left hand
and grabs Mark's weapon hand with
his right hand

Stick Vs. Stick Technique #3

3 - Mike swings Mark's hand down to the six o'clock position Mike places Mark's stick on his triceps

4 - Mike swings his stick simultaneously disarming Mark

5 - And striking his mid section

6 - Mike follows up with a forehand strike to the face.

Felix and Marc square off.

1 - Marc swings a forehand strike. Felix
counter strikes and...

2a - Flips his stick around

2b - To the other side of Marc's strike.

3 - Felix chambers for a forehand strike...

4 - And strikes back at Marc.

Felix and Marc square off.

1 - Marc swings a forehand strike.

2 - Felix evades Marc's strike...

Stick Vs. Stick Technique #5

3 - And strikes Marc's leg.

1 - Phil gives Ron a high forehand strike. Ron zones his body away from the strike and hits Phil's hand.

2 - Phil continues with a high backhand strike at Ron, Ron zones again and strikes Phil's hand.

3 - Phil throws a low forehand strike, this time Ron has to angle his stick over Phil's incoming strike to hit Phil in the hand without being hit himself.

4 - Phil swings a low backhand that Ron picks up by meeting the force of the blow.

KALI EMPTY HAND VS. STICK DRILL

Training Realistically

Phil uses the forearm and hand guard to enhance Ron's training.

5 - Ron has to move his body out of the way of Phil's thrust and returns a strike to Phil's hand.

Ron and Mark square off

1 - Mark swings a forehand strike at Ron

2 - Ron grabs onto Mark's weapon hand with his left hand...

KALI EMPTY HAND VS. STICK DRILL

Empty Hand Defense Against A Stick

3 - And swings it around to his right hand

4 - Ron disarms Mark with his right hand

5 - Ron hits Mark in the head with a forearm strick.

 Mike and Mark square off

1 - Mark swings a forehand strike at Ron,
Ron counters with an eye jab

2 - Ron disarms Mark's stick...

"Snake Disarm"

3 - By slapping Mark's arm off the stick

4 - Ron grabs the stick out from under his arm

5 - Ron grabs the stick out from under his arm

6 - Ron returns a backhand hit to Marc's head.

Ron and Mark square off

1 - Mark chambers his strike
    to the backhand side

2 - Mark swings a backhand strike at Ron,
    Ron counters by placing his left forearm
    on Marc's right forearm

3 - Ron pressures Marc's arm down and to
    the opposite side of his body and places
    the stick on his left forearm

Kali Empty Hand Vs. Stick Drill

Reverse "Snake Disarm"

4 - Ron scoops his arm around the stick.

6 - Ron locks Mark's arm

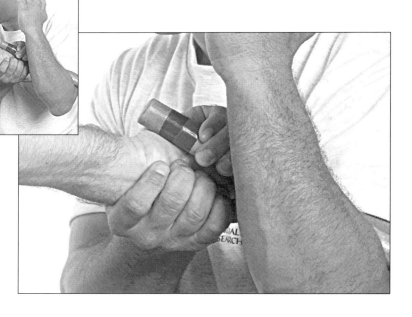

7 - Ron disarms the stick by twisting his body

8 - and strikes Marc in the head

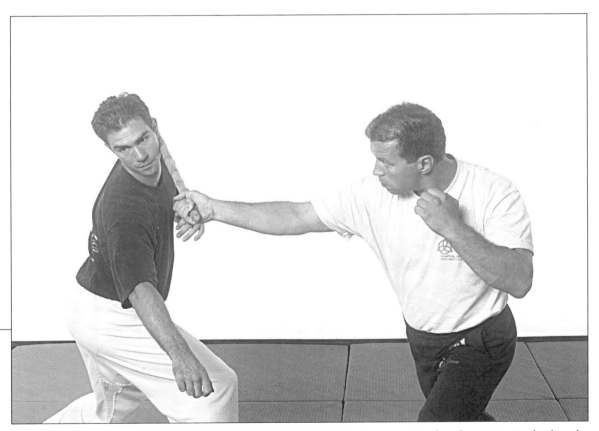

9 - And strikes Marc in the head.

KALI EMPTY HAND VS. KNIFE DRILL

Knife Vs. Knife Drills

1 - Lynn and Phil square off. Lynn places the knife over his head geared to swing at Phil's first movement

2 - Phil starts to move in and Lynn swings a hard downward strike at Phil.

1 - Lynn and Phil square off. Lynn places the knife over his head geared to swing at Phil's first movement

2 - Phil moves out of the way of Lynn's strike

3 - Phil comes back in at Lynn. Lynn covers and slashes upward on Phil's arm

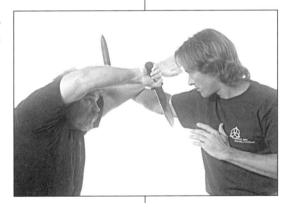

4 - Lynn arm wraps and locks Phil's arm and holds Phil at bay.

Mike and Ron face off

1 - Mike initiates at Ron, Ron turns and runs

JEET KUNE DO - THE PRINCIPLES OF A COMPLETE FIGTHTER

KALI EMPTY HAND VS. KNIFE DRILL

Empty Hand Vs. Knife Technique #1

2 - Ron's out of there and Mike is left behind.

Mike and Ron face off

1 - Ron passes the knife with his forearm from the outside

2 - Ron grabs Mike's knife hand with his right hand (securing the padding of the thumb will limit your opponents mobility)

KALI EMPTY HAND VS. KNIFE DRILL

Empty Hand Vs. Knife Technique #2

3 - Ron pulls Mike's arm maintaining the grip on Mike's knife hand

4 - Ron pushes the knife back at Mike's body

5 - Ron disarms the knife

6 - Ron hyper extends Mike's arm

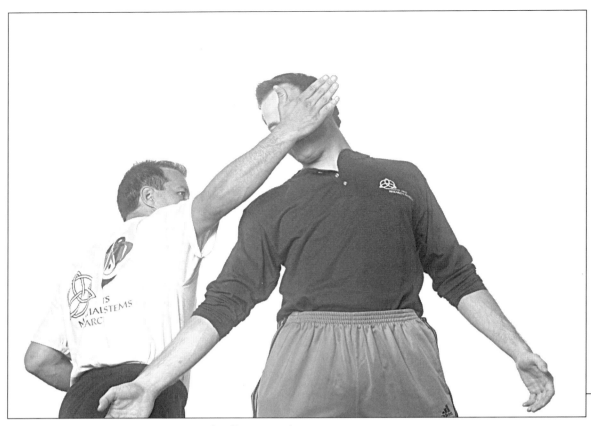

7 - Turns the opposite direction and stiff arms Mike

8 - Ron hooks Mike.

Mike and Ron face off

1 - Ron uses his right forearm to block Mike's forehand slash with the knife

2 - Ron passes the knife past him by applying pressure downward as Mike tries to cut Ron's stomach

Empty Hand Vs. Knife Technique #3

3 - Ron grabs Mike's knife hand. Ron brings Mike's knife hand up so the knife is pointing up; Ron places his and on the flat of the knife

4 - Ron disarms the knife

5 - Ron sets to elbow Mike

6 - Then Ron elbows Mike in the face.

7 - Ron grabs Mike by the back of the head

8 - And knees Mike in the face.

Mike and Ron face off; Mike has the knife in a reverse grip

1 - Mike pulls his arm back to stab

2 - Ron throws keys at Mike's face

KALI EMPTY HAND VS. KNIFE DRILL

Empty Hand Vs. Knife Technique #4

3 - Mike backs off trying to dodge the object thrown at him. Ron follows the keys in and locks the knife with the flat of the blade against his arm and eye jabs Mike

4 - Ron inserts his arm on the outside of Mike's arm

5 - Ron simultaneously eye jabs Mike and disarms him

6 - Ron grabs Mike and stabs Mike in the kidney.

 Ron and Mike face off

1 - Mike draws the knife back to stab Ron

2 - Ron spits at Mike

Empty Hand Vs. Knife Technique #5

3 - Ron grabs Mike's knife hand

4 - Ron disarms Mike

5 - And stabs Mike.

4 — OPTIONS

I love martial arts movies. In some sense, Bruce Lee's magic on the screen is what pulled me into the study of martial arts to begin with. But at the same time, the martial arts fight scenes we all love present an extreme and deceptive picture. Squaring up for the hand-to-hand confrontation should be your last option. Do anything to avoid a fight. Let's face it, in a fight someone gets hurt, and it will likely be you. Even if you are "victorious", the chance of coming out of the fight in one piece is not always that great. In the movies people walk away from a knife wound with a spring in their step. In reality, you do not walk away. As such, it behooves us to consider all of our options.

I am not embarrassed to say that, in a fight, your tennis shoes are your best friend. For goodness sakes, go ahead and run. Live to fight another day by staying in one piece. Today's world is not a world of chivalry and honor. It is a world of emergency rooms and surgery. Avoid that. Your first option should always be to "get away". If that means "running away", then by  all means. It is all well and good to discuss street fighting in the security of your martial arts school or around the table at the pub. But in the streets, there is no honor in death or serious bodily injury. Survival is all that counts.

Of course, getting away is not always an option. That is why we learn to fight. But we need to think, for the moment, beyond hands and feet, beyond the fight itself. Tactics can allow one to prevail - often without a punch or a kick. Let me take a moment to just toss out a few strategic options.

As any martial arts instructor will tell you, avoiding danger is the best way to beat danger. Be aware of your surroundings. Don't park in the dimly lit parking garage. Be aware of the people who are around you. Don't assume that you are safe: make sure of it. Stay out of danger by being aware of potential threats and

evading them in the first instance. This may not seem all that controversial. But the greatest wisdom lies in the obvious. And it is the obvious that we usually ignore.

Your first line of defense, when the situation cannot be avoided centers on what I like to call "the interview". What kind of attitude do you take in a confrontation? I like to tell students in my rape prevention programs not to be a victim by not acting like one. Predators look for weakness. Most predators, and this is generally true in the animal kingdom, look for an easy target. The predator wants the simplest prey with the least risk of injury. Hence, an assailant is best met with a show of confidence. Confidence, strength and attitude will stop many attackers before the attack begins. If they see conviction, if they hear a barrage of verbal "in your face" abuse, they often will go no further.

Be aware of space. Obstructions can be a beautiful thing. Put a car, a fire hydrant, a mailbox, in between you and the assailant. Use space strategically. By being conscious of the things that are around you, you can keep a safe distance and even create an escape route for yourself.

Physical space will often determine strategy. In some cases, having a lot of space between you and the attacker is a good sort of thing. Space can allow you the jump you need to escape. But space is not always a good sort of thing. When faced with multiple attackers, a wall to your back may keep you from being surrounded. Further, you don't have to be Jackie Chan to use whatever is lying about. Jackie may be the best in the movies at taking anything lying around and making it into a weapon. But this is not all that hard a thing to do. Be aware of what is around you and use it to your best advantage.

Elements of your environment may be used to cover or conceal. For concealment, you can hide behind objects or screen yourself from view. To cover is a different sort of thing. A piece of cardboard will conceal you from attack but it will not shield you from harm. A wall will stop a bullet, a trash can lid will

stop a knife. You may cover and you may conceal. To hide and to shield are different things, but each must be kept in mind.

Be on the lookout for unseen weapons. Weapons are often concealed. The assailant might have a weapon, the assailant may have a previously unseen friend (which is as good as a weapon), or the assailant may have a friend with a weapon. These are all things to be looked for in the interview stage.

You yourself may have a weapon. The knife is a great equalizer. It can put a woman on even footing with a much larger man. It can put one person on even footing with multiple attackers. But be careful. It may or may not be a wise thing to show the weapon. It may not be a good idea to use the weapon.

Everything around you can be of use. Projectiles of all sorts can be thrown or used to strike the assailant. They can create a diversion, provide cover, conceal, or used to strike. Awareness of your environment, awareness of your options, given the physical circumstances, can save your life.

During the 90's, the great grapplers of the West argued vociferously that one could never deal with multiple attackers. After all, if going to the ground is your only option then this might be true. But it is not. If any instructor said to me that, when faced with multiple attackers you might as well give up - there is nothing you can do - I would find another teacher. Giving up, in terms of thinking and working to find a solution, is not an option. And it is not necessary. The myth that one cannot deal with multiple attackers is just that, a myth. It is certainly not an easy, or preferable, situation. But there are options.

Indeed, in some sense JKD manifests itself most patently in the multiple opponent scenario. Dealing with more than one aggressor takes spontaneity. There is no way to pre-plan. When facing one opponent you may think to yourself, "first I am going to slant right and jab, then I will follow with a...". In this manner the relaxed, "let it come out" attitude we work so  hard to cultivate in JKD gets lost. Learning to let go is the hardest thing to do. However, when faced with more than one opponent, there is no option. Sifu Dan Inosanto used to liken this situation to the broken play in football. As a former gridiron hero, Sifu Dan tends to express these ideas in terms of the creative, play it as it goes, scenario one finds in a football mistake. When something on offense goes wrong, when the pre-set play fails, the quarterback, or running back, must improvise - find the hole, hit the open man. This kind of free flowing mindset, the ability to see and feel the opening, is the first requirement when you are by yourself and facing more than one opponent. And this is perhaps the most honest expression of JKD.

1 - Mike and Mark face off against Ron

2 - Mike and Mark start to come in at Ron; Ron starts to sector to his right

3 - Ron places Mark in-between he and Mike

Flexibility and adjusting to the "broken play" must be complimented by a clear focus. You cannot afford to get distracted. This operates much like driving a car. When you drive, your mind really is on automatic. You focus on the road and the peripheral distractions are left aside. There are multiple distractions - kids playing, other cars, work crews, etc,. When all is going well you can ignore these things. However, if a child runs into the street, or if another car swerves into your path, you change your focus. Facing multiple opponents takes this same kind of focus and flexibility.

When facing more than one opponent, a straight line can be a beautiful thing. Positioning is everything. To be sure, you never want to let yourself get surrounded. Fundamentally, though, when you are one facing two or three, your best advantage lies in keeping them in a straight line. It is not hard to see how their advantage is lost, at least temporarily, if only one of them has you in reach. This allows you, in one strategy, to hit the lead assailant hard, and run. Keep them lined up. Stop quickly and strike the lead assailant. Repeat as necessary. Obviously you must be in good condition to do this.

Two on two fighting is an interesting process. Here one can, and indeed must, plan. Success in multiple fighting depends largely on how well you know your partner. You must be able to play off of your partner's strengths and cover for his or her weaknesses. The strategy you use will depend on these variables. If your partner is slow and less mobile, you can criss-cross and double back around the other team in a flanking type of movement. In this way, assuming that your partner can stand his ground, you can get behind the assailants and strike from a position of advantage. Proper multiple fighting takes prior planning, strategy, and a good sense of your partner's abilities.

Weapons, of course, can even out a fight. An armed fighter, who really knows how to use the weapon, can often take on more than one person without exces-

sive difficulty. A knife will allow you to disable one attacker before you must face the other. This works particularly well with the "line them up" approach advocated above. If you can line them up, disable the front assailant with a weapon attack, then run and reline them up again, you can succeed. A weapon, a stick, a knife, any blunt instrument, can even the odds - perhaps even shift them in your favor.

3B - Ron places Mark in-between he and Mike

There is no question that you can survive a multiple opponent situation. It is the without doubt the hardest thing to do. Strategy, tactics, conditioning, and training are essential. Focus and flexibility are a must. But it can be done. With the proper training and the proper mindset, you can come out on top when faced with more than one assailant.

MULTIPLE OPPONENT DRILLS

2 Vs. 2 Criss Cross Drill

A1

B1

Phil and Ron square off against Mike and Mark
(Phil is in the far left, Ron is in the white T-shirt)

A2

B2

As the fighters start to engage at each other...

A3

B3

Ron crosses over and attacks Mike; Ron goes for
Mike but still tries to make Mark come in at him

A4

B4

Phil criss crosses over and hits Mark while his attention is diverted

MULTIPLE OPPONENT DRILLS

2 Vs. 2 The Run Away & Return

A1

B1

Phil and Ron square off against Mike and Mark
(Phil is in the far left, Ron is in the white T-shirt)

A2

B2

As the fighters start to engage at each other...

A3

Phil runs away, Mike goes after him, Ron crosses over and hits Mike

B3

A4

Mark starts to attack Ron...

B4

A5

Phil returns from behind hitting Mike while he is distracted

B5

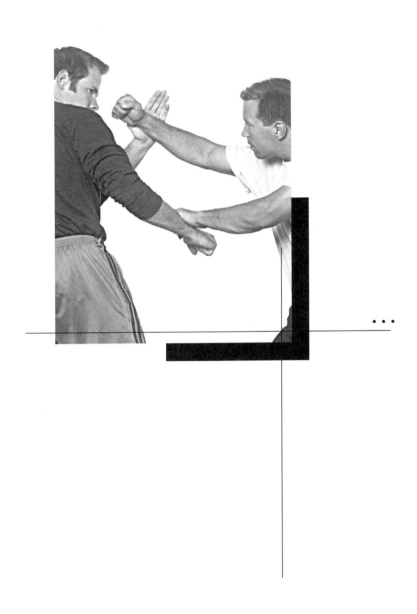

...

6 ——— TRAPPING

Bruce Lee absorbed hand trapping from a variety of systems. Wing Chun Gung Fu, Pencak (pronounced (Penchak) Dutch/Indonesian spelling Pentjak) Silat, Escrima, and other arts influenced his approach to trapping. One system you may not believe that Bruce Lee drew trapping from was European fencing. Bruce's brother, Peter was a champion fencer in Hong Kong. Peter would play a game with Bruce of hand fencing. The brothers would square off and start to probe with their hands as if they were fencing foils, one would try to score with a strike while the other would try to misguide the blow and counter attack. Indeed fencing is a large part of JKD if you were to look at the Tao of Jeet Kune Do you would find many fencing terms such as ABD (attack by draw), ABC (attack by combination), SIA (single indirect attack) and PIA (progressive indirect attack). Bruce would also use fencing terms like the beat, bind, envelope, pressure and the croise. All of which were used as manipulations and are fencing terms. (135)

What is trapping? In the book Wing Chun Gung-Fu: Chinese Art of Self-Defense, by J. Yimm Lee (Bruce Lee being the technical editor), under the chapter, "Trapping Hands", trapping is described as, "Immobilizing an opponent's hands...[In Wing Chun this] is called phon sao. Literally translated 'phon' means to seal or to close off an object or area...the English word, immobilize, is probably the best translation of phon." It is my opinion that trapping is essential in martial arts, in sport or real-life combat. It is only one of a myriad of tools used in the martial arts arsenal, to be sure. However, being able to immobilize an opponent's hand(s) provides obvious advantages. If an opponent's hands are pinned to his or her body, then he or she cannot respond.
One of the most important elements of trapping is the centerline theory. The cen-

terline is an imaginary line between you and your opponent that always connects the two combatants. Imagine a nail sticking out of the top of yours head and one

A: Biu Da

B: Jong Da

C: Tan Da

similarly sticking out of your opponent's head. Now imagine a string connected to each of the protruding nails. No matter how you move in the circle, you and your opponent will always have that line between you. That is the centerline. Now, imagine your opponent facing you and blocking your punch like a boxer would, slightly pawing at the blow, not really passing the center of his own face with his hand while moving his head just enough to avoid the blow. This would be considered by JKD to be inside the centerline. Then, think of a hard block like you might find in Karate, where the blocker uses his forearm or hand to block the blow pushing past his face. The JKD player would consider this block to be past the centerline. Either a soft or a hard block would not stop an experienced JKD practitioner. One defense is not better than the other to JKD - it would only send him or her down a different path.

Recently, a controversy has bubbled up about the value of trapping in a real fight. Some people in the JKD community say that trapping is not effective in a real altercation. This is just manifestly false. One answer makes the argument. They say, "why haven't we seen trapping in the Ultimate Fighting Championship (UFC) - the most realistic form of sparring?" The answer...we have. I'm not referring here to a fighter who strictly uses trapping as his singular fighting style. Rather, if you were to examine almost any bout in a UFC match, you will see some form of trapping, what Bruce Lee called "hand immobilization" regardless of how crude. The clinch is a trap. Grabbing the opponent's arms is a trap. In sum, a richer, more fundamental definition of the concept "trapping" shows clearly how traps are endemic to real situations.

Others have said that it takes too long to become effective in the use of trapping. Well, what is "too long"? Trapping is a delicate art that takes time to fully appreciate. And yet, it seems that in today's society, we want everything fast. We are accustomed to fast food, fast information on the Internet, fast banking and fast relationships. Like anything worthwhile, trapping does not come easy; it requires a lot of time and dedication. If trapping is not for you, then maybe there is an art out there that will give you quicker success. After all, the JKD way is to "...use what works for you and discard what doesn't, and what doesn't work for you may work for another". Perhaps one can do well with a quick fix. I doubt it. But for the majority in the JKD world, we will always enjoy the benefits of trapping that comes only from years of hard training.

Trapping has an important place in the use of Jun Fan equipment training. The realistic element of focus mitt training allows for full speed trapping combined with all out power. Employing focus mitts while trapping may feel clumsy at first. However, like riding a bike, the more you do it, the better you will be at it. Keep it simple at first. As you begin to master the basic motions you'll soon begin adding to it, creating a detailed workout that is tailor-made for you. Although trapping can be at times intricate and complex, it does have its place in focus mitt training.

Trapping is everywhere. Immobilizing an opponent's limbs, trapping the extremity, happens. If you immobilize you stop the attack; if you trap you can't get hit. Working trapping drills develops timing, sensitivity, and body awareness. For these reasons I will continue to work and to teach the seemingly arcane drills that provide the long-term payoff in trapping skills.

Ron and Sifu Dan face off

1 - Sifu Dan jabs; Ron parries the jab and hits to the body

2 - Ron goes from the low hit to the high back hand strike (Chop Choy Gua Choy)

3 - Ron inside traps Sifu Dan's hand and strikes (Loy Pac Sao Da)

JEET KUNE DO - THE PRINCIPLES OF A COMPLETE FIGTHTER

TRAPPING ON THE FOCUS MITTS

Trapping Drill Series 1

4 - Sifu Dan inside blocks Ron's arm

5 - Ron swings his arm in a clockwise motion to a backhand strike (Lau Sing Choy) Sifu Dan blocks

6 - Ron uses an eye jab; Sifu Dan's arm blocks Ron's strike

7 - Ron pulls Sifu Dan's arm down and strikes (Lop Sao)

8 - Ron crosses

9 - Ron body hooks

10 - Ron grabs on to Sifu Dan's neck
and gears back

11 - And knees.

 Ron and Sifu Dan face off

1 - Sifu Dan jabs; Ron parries the jab and hits to the face

2 - As Sifu Dan's hand comes in to block Ron swings his arm in and

3 - Up to a backhand strike

4 - Ron then eye jabs and Sifu Dan blocks

5 - Ron pulls Sifu Dan arm (Lop Sao) and

6 - Backhand strikes (Gua Choy)

8 - Ron crosses

9 - Uppercuts

10 - Crosses and...

11 - Round kicks the leg (Now Tek).

. . .

7 ——— GOING TO THE GROUND

Previously in this book you heard me say that some ground fighting schools act as though the ground is the only place one will ever fight. I have been clear that this is not the case. But make no mistake, many, if not most, fights will go to the ground. Ignoring ground fighting, as many traditionalists do, is hazardous to your health. The classic martial arts training method, where the opponent is thrown to the ground, hit once and the fight is "over", is anything but realistic. Ground fighting is not that simple.

Ground fighting may not always be preferable, but most of the time no one is asking our opinion. I lived much of my life in Chicago. The streets tend to get snowy, icy, muddy, wet, and generally exhibit other unpleasant conditions. (perhaps this is why I moved to California!) In these kinds of conditions, keeping your footing is rarely an easy thing to do. Fights often go to the ground because the ground itself demands it.

Probably the single most important aspect to ground fighting is conditioning. Ground fighting is a marathon. I've seen highly conditioned distance runners get completely winded in 30 seconds of grappling. Weight lifters have the hardest time. Body builders tend to condition themselves for failure. They will try to push that last rep hard until they quit and cant' lift any longer. When you grapple a weight lifter you can feel him pushing hard to get that last rep in. Then he collapses, just as he does after finishing that last repetition. If you can hold out while they push you can feel the failure coming. Grappling is like swimming. You use every muscle. So, conditioning and endurance are everything on the ground.

Proper ground training generates a sensitivity identical to that created in stand up sensitivity drills like chi sao. Unlike the hand drills, grappling builds body sensitivity. As you hold off the opponent you can feel where he or she is going. This allows you to manipulate the positioning until you get what you want. If you feel the attack coming you can muffle or nullify the blow before it becomes a problem. When you feel a movement towards a technique you can anticipate the attack and counter. Make no mistake; ground fighting is as delicate and sensitive a side to the art as punching and kicking.

Punching on the ground is extremely important. Most people will strike in a grappling situation. However, they usually do it without any force. To effectively punch, particularly from the top position, you need to rise up and twist the body. You drop your weight forward just like a stand up punch. Instead of dropping the hip, twisting the foot and shoulder in the way a stand up punch works, punching on the ground requires greater upper body control and a greater use of the torso in generating the drop and twist needed to effectively strike. This actually helps develop the attributes necessary for better stand up punching as well.

I like to drill this with a "fist suit" similar to the police Redman suit. It has rib padding - looking something like the Michelin man - as well as a helmet. Students can really punch at me from the ground. I can then swing back and a real ground grappling punching scenario can be trained. Often I will lie on my back holding Thai pads and let the student attack the body. I may hold the pads backwards and let them hit me in the ribs. This conditions real ground fighting with full contact punching.

Training in this manner not only pushes the envelope on ground striking, but it trains the student to watch out for a lock. When you flail pitifully the opportunity for an arm lock is real. You give an opponent the opportunity to finish the fight when a punch has no meaning. Just because someone is the aggressor, just because someone is punching furiously, does not mean that person has an advantage. A flailing limb is a lock waiting to happen. Hence, learning to punch properly on the ground is a defensive necessity as well as an offensive advantage.

Wrestling alone won't win a fight. You need to be aggressive and you need to strike. But when you strike you must do so effectively. In the streets they don't count points; they don't give you extra credit for aggressive effort and there is no referee to stop the fight if you are in serious trouble. A strike must have power and it must not leave you open for a lock. Trained properly, striking from the ground will add the extra element needed to win.

As a final note, learning to fight on the ground is essential for women. Assailants typically will struggle with a woman on the ground. As important as it is, though, women tend to shy away from ground fighting instruction. It should not be surprising that most women are uncomfortable with having big sweaty men get on top of them in practice. So it is  incumbent on the instructor to find a way to help women learn by creating a safe and encouraging environment.

GROUND FIGHTING DRILLS
Thai Pad Drill

5 - Pushes Mike an...

4 - Knees

6 - Ends with a right round kick.

Ron and Mark face off

1 - Ron left round kicks

3 - Ron elbows

2 - Mike crosses; Ron parries Mike's cross

GROUND FIGHTING DRILLS

Thai Elbow Drill - Empty Handed

1 - Ron and Mike face off

2 - Mike slaps Ron's arm out of the way

3 - Ron arm collapses into an elbow strike.

GROUND FIGHTING DRILLS
Thai Boxing Elbow Drill - Focus Mitts

1 - Ron and Mike face off

2 - Mike slaps Ron's arm out of the way

3 - Ron arm collapses into an elbow strike.

This drill can be performed
right and left handed.

Phil comes towards Diana

1 - Diana drops

2 - Phil tries to grab Diana

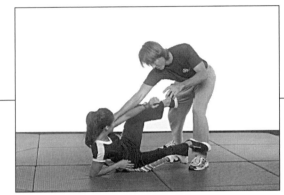

3 - Diana kicks Phil in the groin

GROUND FIGHTING DRILLS
Malphilindo Silat - Defending From The Ground

4 - Diana kicks Phil's leg as he tries to place it on the ground

5 - Diana shifts to her left hip and...

6 - Traps Phil's leg

7 - And kicks Phil to the ground

8 - Diana gets up and...

9

10 - Runs away.

From the ground position Diana places her legs in a chambered ready position

Diana kicks the groin, then A, B, C, D, or E.

A - Diana uses her foot to take down Phil.

B - She uses her shin.

C - She uses her hand.

D - She uses her shoulder.

GROUND FIGHTING DRILLS
Variations Of Defending From The Ground

E - She swings her leg over and scissor locks Phil's leg and takes him down.

GROUND FIGHTING DRILLS

Getting Up Safely From The Ground
The Wrong Way

1 - Ron and Marc demonstrate the wrong way to try and stand while in a fight

2 - Ron leans forward trying to get up

3 - Marc hits Ron because he is too close.

GROUND FIGHTING DRILLS
Getting Up Safely From The Ground
The Right Way

1 - Ron demonstrates the correct way to handle an attacker. He keeps Marc off him by sticking his arm out

2 - Ron posts his left arm on the ground and swings his left leg back

3 - Ron stands while having a defense up.

1 - Ron holds on to Marc's leg

2 - Ron releases Marc's leg and falls backward

3 - Ron thrusts upward kicking into Marc's focus mitts

GROUND FIGHTING DRILLS

Training From The Ground With Equipment

4 - Ron drops to Marc's opposite leg

5 - Ron grabs on to Marc's leg ready to do the drill from the reverse side.

Ron starts with his guard up

1 - Ron rolls over

2 - Ron kicks from the ground position

3 - After the kick Ron retracts his right leg

4 - And brings his left leg back still holding his guard up

GROUND FIGHTING DRILLS
Training From The Ground With Equipment

5 - Ron stands still holding his guard up.

GROUND FIGHTING DRILLS

Thai Boxing Grabbing The Neck
The Wrong Way

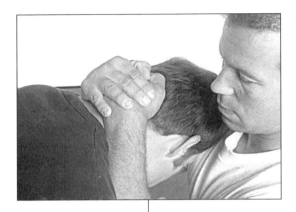

1A - Grabbing the neck the wrong way. Ron grabs Mike by the base of the neck.

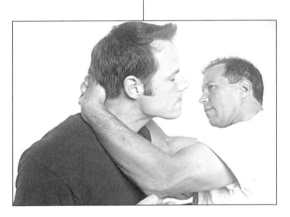

1B - Mike forces his head up. In this position Ron cannot hold Mike's head down.

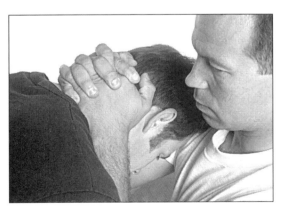

2 - In this picture Ron places his fingers in jeopardy by lacing them together. If Mike twists his head quickly it could break Ron's fingers.

Thai Boxing Grabbing The Neck
The Right Way

1 - Grabbing the neck the correct way. Ron grabs Mike the correct way by placing his arm along the side of Mike's neck knife hand with his right hand

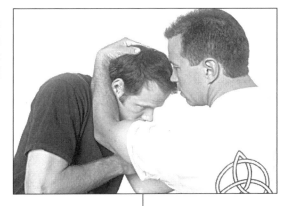

2 - Ron grabs his wrist and squeezes his forearms together

3 - Ron knees Mike.

GROUND FIGHTING DRILLS

Thai Boxing Switch Knee

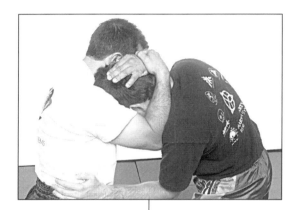

1 - Ron grabs Mike by the neck

2 - Ron knees Mike's body. Mike tries to stop Mike's knee with his forearm

3 - Ron switches knees.

GROUND FIGHTING DRILLS

Defending Against The Knee
The Wrong Way

1 - Mike stops Ron from kneeing him with the palms of his hands

2 - Ron twists his hip and makes Mike's hands slip off Ron's hip

3 - Ron delivers a knee to Mike's body.

1 - Ron tries to knee Mike; Mike stops Ron by barring his fists into Ron's hip

2 - Ron tries to twist his hip to shake Mike's hands off of his hips. He fails

3 - Ron tries to knee Mike. Mike successfully stops Ron

4 - Mike pulls Ron close to his body, bending Ron backward making it hard to knee

GROUND FIGHTING DRILLS
Defending Against The Knee
The Right Way

5 - Mike returns a knee to Ron's ribs.

Ron tries to knee Mike. Mike successfully defends with a forearm block

A

A1 - Ron twists Mike's head

A2 - Curve knees Mike in the face.

A3

B

B1 - Ron delivers an elbow to Mike's face.

GROUND FIGHTING DRILLS
Four Methods To Counter Knee Defenses

C

D

C1 - Ron comes back with a low kick to Mike's leg.

D1 - Ron retracts is leg

D2 - Ron lifts his knee over Mike's arm and

D3 - Wipes his knee down Mike's face.

Mike round kicks Ron

A

A1 - Mike fakes high and kicks low.

GROUND FIGHTING DRILLS

Defending Against The Kick
The Wrong Way

B1 - Ron's hands were not high enough to protect him from Mike's kick.

Mike round kicks Ron

A

A1 - Ron covers the kick.

B

B1 - Ron knees Mike's thigh.

GROUND FIGHTING DRILLS

Thai Boxing Kick And Counters

C

C1 - Ron cut kicks Mike.

D

D1 - Ron catches Mike's leg

D2 - Ron holds the leg and cut kicks.

Mike round kicks Ron

E

A1 - Ron foot jabs Mike.

F

F1 - Ron ducks Mike's kick

F2 - Ron shoots forward grabbing Mike's leg

F3 - Ron takes Mike down.

 Ron and Marc face off

 1 - Ron switches his stance ready to kick Marc

 2 - Ron kicks Marc; Marc catches Ron's foot under his arm...

 3 - And kicks Ron's support leg

 4 - Ron goes down to the ground

5 - Marc stands and applies an Achilles lock to Ron's ankle

7 - Ron kicks at Marc; Marc
    parries the kick...

8 - Marc pushes Ron's foot over
    his leg and places his leg
    over Ron's leg trapping it

9 - Marc sits down squeezing his legs together and applies an Achilles lock on Ron.

Ron and Marc face off

1 - Ron switches his stance ready
    to kick Marc

2 - Ron kicks Marc; Marc catches Ron's foot
    under his arm...

3 - And kicks Ron's support leg

Catch Kick To Achilles Lock Counter

4 - Ron goes down to the ground

5 - Marc stands and applies an
Achilles lock to Ron's ankle

6 - Ron hooks his arm around Marc's leg

7 - Ron weaves his leg around Marc's leg...

8 - And takes Marc down to the ground

9 - Ron squeezes his knees together holding Marc's leg in position...

10 - And applies a heel hook hold.

Ron and Marc face off

1 - Ron kicks Marc; Marc covers and...

2 - Goes into double leg tackle Ron

3 - Marc lifts Ron and...

4 - Drops him to the ground

Tackle To Achilles Lock Counter

5 - Marc grabs Ron's ankle

6 - Marc stands and puts an Achilles lock on Ron; Ron stops Marc's motion by kicking into Marc's hip

7 - Ron puts his leg in between Marc's legs

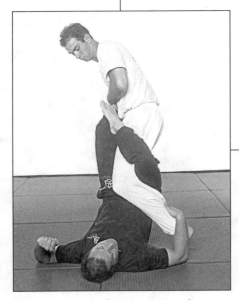

8 - Ron weaves his Leg around
    Marc's leg

9 - Ron twists his body on the
    ground forcing Marc to fall

10 - Ron applies a heel hold lock on Marc.

Ron and Marc face off

1 - Ron jabs at Marc and Marc parries and...

2 - Body tackles Ron

3 - Ron rolls his forearm across Marc's face

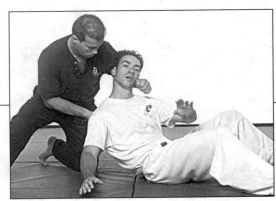

4 - Ron rolls Marc over onto his back

Tackle Counter To A Neck Crank

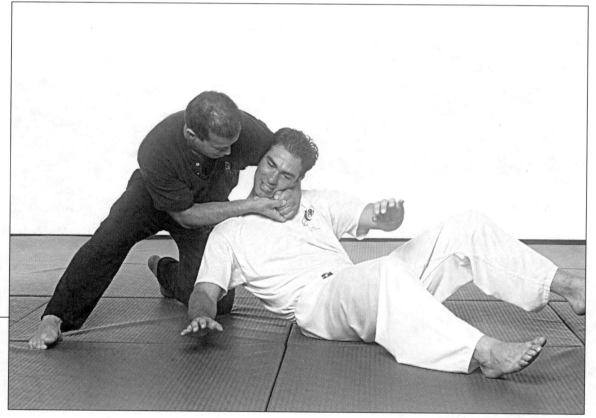

5 - Ron puts Marc in a neck crank.

 Ron and Marc face off

 1 - Ron kicks Marc; Marc covers and...

2 - Marc tries to double leg
    tackle Ron; Ron uses a
    forearm block to stop Marc
    (very important to have your
    arm bent and elbow down)

Forearm Block

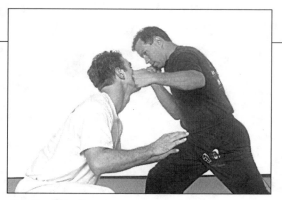

3 - Ron hooks...

4 - Crosses...

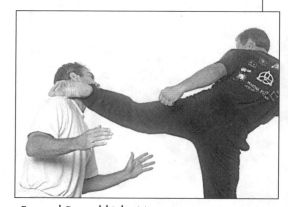

5 - and Round kicks Marc.

Mark holds the Thai pads for Ron

1 - Ron throws a right round kick into the pad

2 - Marc tries to body tackle Ron; Ron grabs Marc's neck and back of head

3 - Ron uppercuts the pad

4 - Crosses

Equipment Training The Forearm Block

5 - Round kicks.

Mike is in Ron's guard position

1 - Mike punches Ron; Ron
    bends his body at the waist
    and parries the punch

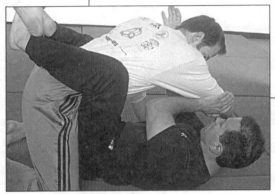
2 - Ron wraps his arm around Mike's neck

3A - Ron puts Mike in a front sleeper choke

JEET KUNE DO - THE PRINCIPLES OF A COMPLETE FIGTHTER

Shoot Wrestling From The Guard

3B - If Mike blocks the choke Ron kicks his
legs out extending Mike's legs

4 - Ron kicks up

5 - And turn Mike over

8 - After the turn over Ron dismounts still retaining the hold on Mike's neck

9 - Ron slides his knee...

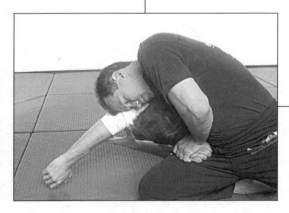

10 - Under Mike's neck

11 - Ron puts Mike into a side body guillotine.

GROUND FIGHTING DRILLS

Juan Gern Entry To Rear Choke

5 - Pushes on Mike's lower back

4 - Ron wraps his arm around Mike's neck

6 - Ron puts a rear choke on Mike.

Ron and Mike face off

1 - Ron jabs; Mike parries

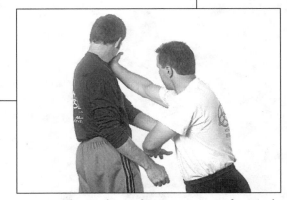

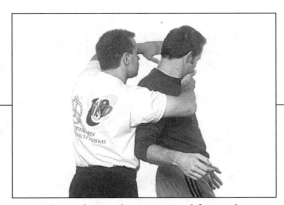

3 - Ron pushes Mike's jaw and forces him to turn

2 - Ron thrusts his palm (Juan Gern) forward

Appendix 1

THE LAW AND YOU

As a martial artist, it is absolutely imperative that you understand the local laws as they apply to you in a fight situation. You may be justified in responding to a threat, but your response itself may be legally unacceptable. Knowing what you are allowed to do can save you an enormous amount of trouble later on. Of course, I am not suggesting that you put yourself at risk. We always like to say that it is better to be tried by twelve than carried by six. Protect your life. But be aware of the local laws that tell you what constitutes an appropriate response.

In California we use what is called the "California Use of Force Chart" (see page 177). Fundamentally, this approach entails that you have the right to use an equal or greater force to stop an assailant from causing great bodily harm or imminent death. If you are threatened with death or bodily injury you can defend yourself. However, once the threat has been met you must stop your attack. If you continue your response once the threat has been neutralized, in the eyes of the law, you become the aggressor. A threat of injury, or even death, does not license all behavior.

Probably the best benchmark for employing an appropriate response is the common sense perspective of proportionality. A punching attack does not merit a knife response. Keep your response at about the same level, or perhaps the minimal necessary level, to neutralize the threat. But once the threat is neutralized, stop. This is not such an easy thing to do. When an assailant succumbs it is not easy to simply "turn it off". Adrenaline, rage, and even fear make stopping the defense difficult. But when it is done it is done. Understand the level of threat you face and respond in proportion.

Unfortunately, the modern martial arts super hero on the screen has given society unrealistic expectations about the things martial artists can do. We are not mystical super heroes who can leap tall buildings in a single bound. At least I'm not. As such, be aware that those judging you might not really understand the threat you face and your ability to deal with that threat.

Of course, at the end of the day, you must consult your own state's regulations to fully understand what constitutes a legally acceptable response to a threat. It is well worth the time.

As we like to say, it is better to be tried by twelve than carried by six.

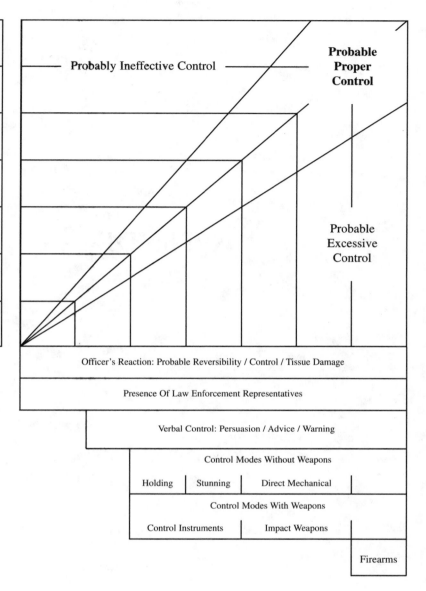

| Subject(s) immediately threaten death or serious physical injury |
| Subject(s) immediately threaten to harm others |
| Subject(s) aggressively offensive without weapons |
| **ACTIVE** Subject(s) actively resist in a defensive manner |
| **PASSIVE** Subject(s) not controlled by verbal direction. Subject(s) resist by not moving |
| Subject(s) cooperative, but must be given directions for compliance |
| Subject(s) appear cooperative |

Probably Ineffective Control

Probable Proper Control

Probable Excessive Control

Officer's Reaction: Probable Reversibility / Control / Tissue Damage

Presence Of Law Enforcement Representatives

Verbal Control: Persuasion / Advice / Warning

Control Modes Without Weapons

| Holding | Stunning | Direct Mechanical |

Control Modes With Weapons

| Control Instruments | Impact Weapons |

Firearms

APPENDIX 2

WORKING WITH DISABILITIES

Many martial artists work with the disabled. Some do it for the noblest of intentions; some do it as charity. For me, working with lower leg disabilities became a passion almost by accident. A number of my best students, including Steve Gold who is my co-author here, came to me with serious lower leg disabilities. I did not seek this out. However, having had the good fortune to work and adapt with a number of outstanding, motivated, students who have these challenges has taught me a lot about martial arts, and about myself.

Let me take the time, in this addendum, to turn this over to Steve and let him tell you, as a philosopher and martial artist who faces these challenges, just how he sees the middle portion of the wide spectrum of disabilities, how we have come to adapt to them in our training, and what we have learned. After cashing out the conceptual nature of disability in our society, he will, through opening up his own personal experience, attempt to demonstrate that if a partially disabled person finds the right instructor, and focuses on the style best suited to one's limitations and strengths, the disability can be surmounted, and an effective martial style developed. Moreover, those of us fortunate enough not to have these challenges can learn valuable lessons that will help us to adapt to changes forced on us by circumstance.

JUST ANOTHER CHALLENGE

Prejudice comes in so many forms. Race, religion, gender, disability, just about every way one human can find to differentiate from another has been used to oppress or marginalize. As with all bigotry, the categories we use to label the "other" can exhibit either positive or negative qualities. Oddly enough, 'good' attributes can label and be bigoted as well as 'bad' ones. Obviously, referring to a member of an oppressed group as lazy, stupid, greedy, inherently violent, or incapable of taking on responsibility constitute typical negative categories. (I ask the reader to associate such negative attributes with whichever subgroup comes to mind in order to avoid offense) By the same 'token' positive attributes like, "They are all good at sports", "They all have rhythm", or "They know how to make money", etc. are good sorts of things, yet patently offensive when used to describe certain racial or ethnic groups.

The same negative and positive stereotypes are used for the disabled. On the negative side we have all seen Jerry Lewis, for all the good work he has done, cry embarrassingly for the "poor pitiful wretches" who need his help. Characterizing the disabled as ones to be pitied is shameful. From personal experience I can tell you that pity is not only unwelcome, but among the most humiliating things one can experience. By the same 'token' imputing excessively positive attributes to the disabled is equally damaging. Look around you. In today's world the disabled are pictured as heroes, martyrs, and great leaders who have conquered the impossible to rise above us all - an INSPIRATION.

Labeling the disabled as inspirations to all of US, that is, the "normal" people, is no better than treating the disabled as pitiful helpless creatures. Either way we are marginalized. The fact of the matter is that the disabled ARE normal. We differ in no significant way from anyone else. Disability is JUST ONE MORE CHALLENGE!

Everyone faces challenges in his or her life, challenges that can have a substantial material impact on one's ability to train in the martial arts. In the March 1998 issue of IKF Vincent Moore wrote an extremely perspicacious piece on the difficulties of moving to a new town and being forced to keep up his training without a qualified instructor. Talk about a handicap! Though Mr. Moore has some exceptional ideas on how to overcome this impediment, martial arts training is "hands on" and I don't envy his position. I may be "gimpy", but at least I have the good fortune to train privately with Ron Balicki, a world class martial artist who lives only ten minutes from my home. When you think about it, everyone has to adjust his or her martial style to his or her own talents, limitations and other objective constraints. From size, strength, and gender, to location, money and school availability we all have things that make us adjust. Disability is just one more thing to adjust to.

DEGREES OF DISABILITY

The category "disabled" brings to mind extremes. In the martial arts we think of the dramatic case of a person with no arms learning to kickbox or of a powerful Sifu in a wheelchair. These men and women exist and excel; however, they exhibit the extreme. Disability actually admits of a wide degree of variations. From a ripped up knee, crushed leg, or unusable hand to cerebral palsy and more, disabled people come in all shapes and sizes with varying degrees of challenges. Our fixation on the extreme cases does a substantial disservice to those who face moderate disabilities.

Supposedly, reading an article about a guy with a fatal neuromuscular disease who learned Tae Kwon Do will inspire one to work harder. Actually, few can relate to such extreme cases, though, to be sure, such people deserve substantial credit for their discipline and hard work. Their work deserves to be featured for its own merits, not simply because it is inspirational. More to the point, the inability to identify with the far end of the spectrum actually causes many of the moderately disabled to feel guilty and stop training. Our preoccupation with sensational cases tends to make us look upon the moderately disabled as wimps who don't recognize the axiom "no pain no gain". Excuse me, but after 12 surgeries and two years spent re-learning to walk, the relationship of pain to gain is something I am quite familiar with, no matter how "normal" I look.

The fact is, a person who has had his or her leg crushed, or a martial artist with a significant back injury must adjust his or her style, perhaps even begin studying a whole new art, in order to continue training. The macho attitude that the moderately disabled face and the lack of understanding of our challenges, often stops us from training altogether. The martial arts community needs to acknowledge moderate disabilities and open up a dialogue, share success stories, and help to normalize our thinking about disability.

LOWER LEG DISABILITIES

Given that most Asian martial arts systems emphasize kicking, a lower leg injury is obviously a major impediment. About 20 years ago, on my way to the library at UCLA, my motorcycle and I had a disagreement with a pickup truck over right of way. Obviously, he won. Fortunately, I slid on my backpack full of philosophy books. Truly it was the first practical application of Plato's work. Unfortunately, it left me with a crushed left leg, limited use of my left foot, constant chronic pain and a myriad of problems I won't whine about here. Be that as it may, it remains impossible for me to kick, pivot in certain directions, assume deep strong stances and more. And yet, adaptation is possible.

FINDING THE RIGHT SYSTEM

The first thing anyone with a significant disability needs to do is find the right art. Obviously, kickboxing, of any variety, is not the right choice for me. At this

time, Jun Fan/Wing Chun seems to suit my needs well. I train privately with Sifu Ron Balicki of Marital Arts Research Systems. We work as partners to take his vast experience (with Dan Inosanto, Francis Fong, Edgar Sulite, Randy Williams and others), to help create a JF/WC style that will work for me. This is, in many ways the purest expression of JKD philosophy, for who is more concerned

with "absorbing what is useful" than one who is routinely told that he is physically incapable of absorbing martial arts at all.

While forms are the foundation of any Asian martial art, the radical pivoting, jumps and sharp movements commonly employed are basically impossible for me to do. During the two years I worked in Northern Praying Mantis, before coming to Sifu Ron, forms per se were out of the question. However, in JF/WC the basic forms are done in a static position. While it is hard for me

---

to drop deep into the Yee Je Keem Yeung Ma stance of JF/WC, the Siu Leem Tau form itself is easily achieved. The SLT, and Bruce Lee's Ung Mun, are done completely without footwork. Keeping my balance is hard, but that is true for anyone. By shifting my weight in the stance on to my good leg, or by focusing the energy of the stance on my good hip, or the one strong part of my bad leg (namely, the heel), I can keep in the stance to an acceptable level. These basic forms then thoroughly drill my hand techniques without the need to resort to footwork.

The more advanced forms of JF/WC can be learned without the kicks. JF/WC forms incorporate low and mid range kicks and have few pivoting or jumping moves that are beyond my abilities. Deleting these kicks makes possible the Chum Kiu and Biu Jee forms without taking the heart out of the system. Choosing the right art for my limitations, then, allows me to finally experience the joy and discipline of doing my daily forms training, something I doubted would ever be possible.

The same adaptations can be made with the Wing Chun wooden dummy. Standing in a more erect posture with my dummy set a bit higher, I am able to run through all the dummy drills. Sifu Ron has thought hard on how to replace the pivots and kicks in the dummy form with knee strikes and gentle flowing motions. This allows me to work the dummy and work it hard. My footwork is tighter and somewhat limited, but my hand techniques are as good as anyone at my level.

One of my biggest concerns with the dummy comes from the crush injury to the lower leg in particular. Crushed nerves can react violently to even the mildest touch. A slight tap in the wrong place can result in complete loss of function in the foot. So, protecting this vulnerability is of key concern in the way I work out. The beauty of the WC dummy, for me, is the ability to remove the leg portion. This allows me to adapt to dummy work, to train hand speed, create energy packing in the forearms, and use the "protractor effect" of the dummy to correct my angles, without the fear of hitting the open nerves and vulnerable bones in my bad leg. Furthermore, severe leg injuries make cardiovascular workouts inconvenient to say the least. So it should be no surprise that I don't have the words to describe the rush I get from working up a sweat on this ancient piece of home exercise equipment. By finding the art that conforms best, a moderately disabled martial artist can enjoy a good work out and excel at the important fundamentals.

MAXIMIZING YOUR STRENGTHS

It is often the case that a person with a significant disability will develop other strengths beyond what an able-bodied person will normally do. Most people with lower leg disabilities are forced to develop substantial upper body and hand strength to compensate in life's daily tasks. Hence, the rudimentary equipment is there to employ devastating joint locks. Chi'n Na then becomes an outstanding piece of the puzzle for a practitioner with lower leg disabilities. Most of my work in stand up joint locking techniques were done during my two years of Northern Praying Mantis study with Sifu Tony Nguyen. Aside from some minor footwork adjustments, most of the methods for wrist, elbow, and shoulder Chi'n Na are well within my "grasp". Having to develop significant upper body strength to simply get around gives me a natural advantage in applying strong joint locks.

Aside from the natural tendency to develop arm strength where the legs cannot function well, or vice versa, being forced to focus on one element of an art can often take the partially disabled student to higher levels than the able bodied generalist. The time another student spends on kicking I am continuing to work on my hand techniques. Devoting full time to that one element that another student who has the physical luxury of being "well rounded" must work on only part time, allows me to excel at this specialty. This plays well into the martial arts maxim of learning one thing well rather than one thousand techniques poorly. A focused approach to training can not only compensate for a disability, but actually play into the practitioner's strengths.

FOR THE INSTRUCTORS

As to instructors who work with students with a moderate disability I suggest two basic principles be observed:

1. Keep the student's limitations closely in mind. Moderate disabilities are

often hidden or easy to forget about. When a moderately disabled student excels there is a tendency to see him or her as able bodied. Be sensitive to the fact that no matter how well the student performs, a crushed leg, or bad back does not disappear. In the heat of sparring and the business of running a class, it is easy to cause serious damage and set someone back by losing the sense of his or her limitations. Furthermore, keep a close eye on your junior instructors. The master of the school may be humble and sensitive, but that may not be the case for his or her assistants.

2. Initiate sensitivity and watch for denial. Don't wait for the partially disabled student to tap out. The type of person who does not let a crushed leg or bad back keep him or her from working hard at a martial art is likely to be the kind of person to over-push. Furthermore, the disabled often exhibit the classic chip on the shoulder "dammit I am totally normal" form of denial. Watch the student and make him or her take a break. Don't praise your student for pushing the envelope if you don't feel it is right. Sifu Ron excels at watching me work and knowing when I am overdoing it. His objective view affords the sensitivity necessary to keep me from hurting myself. Don't ever let your student, with adrenaline pumping, in full blown denial, cause damage by overdoing it.

As an instructor, you might learn something from adapting your style to the needs of a partially disabled student. For example, if, in a fight, you take a particularly nasty shot to the lower left leg, and find yourself fighting on one foot, well, welcome to my world! Perhaps now all the adaptations you developed for your student with a lower leg disability will come in handy. Think about it, we all know of drunken gungfu. If we can learn from a drunkard why can't we learn from the disabled?

CONCLUSIONS YOUR STRENGTHS

For the student with a moderate disability finding the right teacher is a necessary condition for success. Researching and finding the right style is equally important. Jun Fan/Wing Chun is excellent for a lower leg disability but that may not be the right choice for someone with a crushed hand. Strangely enough, however, if the moderately disabled student works hard to find the right teacher and the right style, the disability can not only be surmounted but also often turned into an advantage.

It is certainly not easy for me to open up and tell aspects of my personal story. But mine is hardly unique. This article is designed to encourage instructors and students in all styles to begin to share stories on how they have modified their art to work for people with moderate disabilities. We have heard much, and should hear more, about the great progress made by martial artists on the far end of the disability spectrum. However, it is now time to normalize disability by talking openly about our successes and failures with people who face physical challenges that are less severe but no less important.

After all of this, if you are not convinced by my claims for a moral imperative to normalize disability in the marital arts, then just remember the saying: the disabled is the only minority group that any one of us can join at any moment.

APPENDIX 3

THE PRINCIPLES

The theory in Jeet Kune Do is simple; bring everything down to its basics. Bruce Lee said, "Jeet Kune Do is simply to simplify". But for some thing to simplify isn't that simple. I know this sounds like an oxymoron but to simplify can sometime be a hard thing to do. To simplify you must first understand what you are taking away from. Bruce Lee also said, "A sculptor must chisel away to reach the true body of work". This is also true about Jeet Kune Do. You must understand a combative system before you start dissecting it. In essences Jeet Kune Do is about the building of attributes. To build an attribute within yourself you must first know your weaknesses. This is not an easy thing to look at. When looking in a mirror what do you see? Is it the same thing the world outside sees? One way to look objectively at yourself in Jeet Kune Do is by testing yourself constantly.

This can be done in a number of methods.

1) Constantly testing yourself by Sparring.

2) Testing reaction time (timing yourself during high stress exercise).

3) Evolving with today's technical advancements in the martial arts and training equipment.

4) You must look at your physical ability and adapt for, Injury, Age, Illness, Physical handicaps, Stature (size, growing up, growing old), Flexibility.

Constant monitoring and adjustments is essential for optimum performance. The JKD fighter must know himself.

EQUIPMENT TRAINING

A) Focus Mitts: Manipulated the right way focus mitts can be brought to a level that the JKD man can experience a high stress workout that can compare to sparring.

B) Thai Pads: Used in Thailand by Thai boxers, although not an original training device that was used by Bruce Lee, Thai pads build power and deliver an excellent anaerobic workout. Another workout that will stress the body to fighting like conditions.

C) Wooden Dummy: Used in the art of Wing Chun, popularized by Bruce Lee the dummy is always there for you when you are without workout partners. Builds tuff arms teaches you excellent forward pressure and good form.

D) Target: Bruce Lee was a strong believer in striking targets. He would use pads, paper and human targets. Visualization is the key with targets. The advantage paper gives is the explosiveness it brings out in the practitioner. When striking a pad the practitioner will hold back and not release there full power. Most people will not strike some say because of fear of injuring their hands. Whatever the reason paper is an excellent cure. Paper lets the practitioner unload their heaviest blow without fear of damaging themselves.

E) Punching Bags: Heavy Bag, Speed Bag, Double End Bag, etc: Punching bags offer a plethora of advantages, timing, power, flowing motion, etc...

The theory of Jeet Kune Do is to rid yourself of tribal thinking. The JKD man looks for the weaknesses within himself and looks at what the combative world has to offer.

WEAPONS

Dealing with weapons is a hard subject to do honestly. Theorizing and perform-ing untested techniques in a school can instill false confidence and open you up to great bodily harm or imminent death. Most systems do not offer weapons training until the student reaches a high level in their training, many systems do not offer weapons training at all. To deal with weapons on the street at all you need to ask yourself what level are you prepared to go to. Anyone wielding a weapon at you with intent to do bodily harm is at an extreme advantage. When put in a dangerous weapons situation you must commit 100% to try to survive. You may think you know this fact but without proper training and being exposed to the stresses that come with an object being swung at you at times of over 100 miles per hour. The stress amplifies extremely when you add a sharp blade to the situation. The JKD man should acquaint himself with weapon based systems.

OPTIONS

You have to weigh your options to the fullest. One way we do this is what we call the interview.

Jun Fan (Jeet Kune Do) - Inosanto Method

Jun Fan Gung Fu/Jeet Kune Do was created by the late Bruce Lee. In 1964 Sifu Dan Inosanto began his training with Sifu Lee. The art is based on a compilation of 26 different systems.

Filipino Kali - Inosanto Method

Filipino Martial Arts is a compilation of many systems of Kali, Arnis, and Eskrima. The system we study is taught by Guro Dan Inosanto.

Maphilindo Silat - Inosanto Method

Maphilindo Silat and Madjapahit Martial Art was created by Guro Dan Inosanto. The system is a compilation of the Madjapahit, Philippines and the Indonisian Martial Arts.

LAMECO ESKRIMA

Lameco Eskrima - Sulite Method

Lameco Eskrima was created by the late Punong Guro Edgar G. Sulite in 1981. It is a compilation of 5 major and 6 minor systems of Eskrima.

Wing Chun Gung Fu - Williams Method

In Wing Chun Gung Fu we have three influences. Sifu Dan Inosanto, Sifu Francis Fong, and Sifu Randy Williams.

Thai Boxing - Surisute Method

Our system of Muay Thai was brought to the U.S. by Ajarn (Master) Chai Sirisute who was the Bantam Weight Champion of Don Stadium in Thailand.

Shoot Wrestling - Nakamura Method

Shoot wrestling is a blend of Judo, Ju-Jitsu, Catch-As-Catch-Can Wrestling, Sambo, and Muay Thai. It was developed by Satori Sayama in 1983. Yori Nakamura brought it to the U.S. in 1989.

Degerberg Martial Arts - Degerberg Method

The Degerberg method of Martial Arts is a compilation of many system like Western Boxing, Kali, Jun Fan Gung Fu, Judo, Ju-Jitsu, just to name a few. Based in Chicago, Master Fred Degerberg has made it his life's work to giving back in the martial arts. He and his wife, Katie, created one of the largest and best schools in the world.

Contact Pointman Productions for Martial Arts products, equipment, and training videos. www.pointmanproductions.com

To contact Ron Balicki for seminars or questions, write to ron@ronbalicki.com.